Community Radio in India

Community Radio in India

R. Sreedher
Pooja O. Murada
with contributions from
Al-Amin Yusuph

AAKAR

Community Radio in India
R. Sreedher and Pooja O. Murada

This book has been published with the support of UNESCO New Delhi - Cluster Office for Bhutan, India, Maldives and Sri Lanka

First Published 2019

ISBN 978-93-5002-611-3

Published by
AAKAR BOOKS
28 E Pocket IV, Mayur Vihar Phase I
Delhi 110 091 India
aakarbooks@gmail.com

Laser Typeset at
Sakshi Computers, Delhi

Printed at
Saurabh Printers Pvt. Ltd., Greater Noida

Contents

Foreword

India is witnessing an evident transformation in the way information is being consumed. Of course, digital media has shown tremendous growth without hampering the reach of either print or electronic media, but what's even more interesting is the constant rise in the demand for regional and community media its visible impact.

In the concept of communications for development, community media particularly plays an important role. One of the major issues to address in development is to bridge the large information divide; and community radio is by far the most effective medium to share information in the media dark areas, and to the people at the last mile. It is a media the content of their local interests, in their own dialect and language is shared. It can also document and archive for the posterity the dialects, folk songs, history, culture and traditions of communities at a micro level.

Inspite of the proven effectiveness of community radios the world over, it is still lesser known and has not been used to its full potential in India. There are 242 plus functional community radio stations in India, as of 1st March, 2019; some are at least a decade old; I found there is a lack of formal long term training and accredited recognised community radio broadcaster. It is to fill up this vacuum that we at IIMC set up the Community Radio Empowerment and Resource Centre and Dr. Sreedher has been a constant source of support and inspiration.

This book will be a guide for interested individuals, groups, organizations and students to understand details about the history of community radio in India, governance, community media ethics, who can apply for it and how, guidelines that are to be adhered, types of programs that can be broadcast, how it can be sustained, and the important role that a community plays as a whole along with few case studies. The guide books which are available are almost a decade old. An updated book like this has been long overdue.

I congratulate Dr. Sreedher and Pooja O. Murada for sharing the updates on the policy, and making this book a good guide for students and other interested groups who could make optimum use of this low cost medium—i.e. community radio.

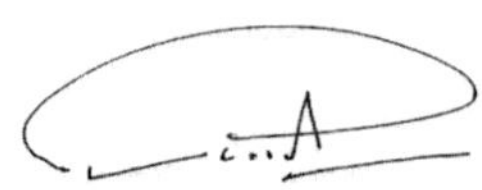

(K.G. Suresh)
Director General
Indian Institute of Mass Communication
(Ministry of Information and Broadcasting, Govt. of India)

Foreword

The writing and publication of this book coincides with two milestones of community broadcasting in India. October 2018 saw the celebration of the tenth anniversary of Sangham Radio at Pastapur in Telangana, which is India's first civil-society-owned community radio station. And on 1 February 2019, Anna Community Radio at Anna University in Tamil Nadu – India's first licensed community radio – completed fifteen years. Looking back over the past decade, the present offers a useful vantage point for assessing how community radio in India continues to be a movement by the people and of the people for the achievement of national and global development goals.

Moreover, *Community Radio in India* is being published at a time when communication and information stakeholders find themselves at a crossroads, both riding the wave of technological progress and grappling with its inherent challenges.

Advances in digital communications continue to bear out the truth of Moore's Law, which – simply put – states that processor speeds or overall processing power for computers will double every two years. Developments in the chip and storage industries have resulted in the application and use of a wide range of information and communication technologies (ICTs), including mobile technology. By 2017 for instance, China and India accounted for a third of global mobile subscriptions. With a mobile penetration rate of 65 per cent, India is expected to add 206 million new mobile subscribers by 2020.[1] With these developments, more and more people are beginning to rely on the Internet to access news and current affairs. For many, the social media have also emerged as a valuable source of information.

Unfortunately, radio has largely been exempt from major advancements in technology, to the extent that pessimists have begun questioning the survival of radio as a medium for the future. The sustainability of radio in its current terrestrial and analogue modes of broadcasting has also been questioned.

While it is undisputable that ICTs have transformed content development and dissemination, they have also introduced a host of challenges, particularly with regard to misinformation and disinformation. The prevalence of these challenges underscores the importance and relevance of curated traditional media such as community radio, which is an extraordinarily effective tool for promoting peaceful, democratic and gender-responsive discourse. Community radio has a proven record of strengthening inclusiveness, diversity, mutual understanding and sensitivity to conflict. Furthermore, the direct engagement between community radio personnel and community members and the exercise of participatory programme development help citizens at the community level acquire media and information literacy.

The United Nations Agenda 2030 calls for concerted efforts to build a peaceful, inclusive, sustainable and resilient future

1. *The Mobile Economy2017*, GSM Association.

for people and the planet. With the adoption of the Sustainable Development Goals (SDGs) and Targets by UN Member States, the latter have pledged to put into place mechanisms to ensure that no one is left behind, and to 'endeavour to reach the furthest behind first'. As the third tier of the broadcast media, community radio is closest to the 'furthest' citizens at the bottom of the pyramid. This is yet another compelling reason for the need for community radio. Indeed, community broadcasting is more relevant today than ever before.

The present book, co-authored by Dr. Sreedher Ramamurthy and Ms Pooja O. Murada, and published by Aakar Books, aims to provide students of journalism and communication and media practitioners with a comprehensive understanding of community radio in India. UNESCO's support for the development of this publication reflects our objective of building peace by promoting the free flow of ideas and encouraging the exchange of knowledge among people through all possible means of mass communication. We are certain that *Community Radio in India* will go a long way towards strengthening young people's understanding of community radio as a vehicle for change; a platform for citizens' self empowerment; and an essential tool for fostering inclusiveness, gender-sensitivity and democratic decision-making.

(Eric Falt)
Director and UNESCO Representative
to Bhutan, India, Maldives and Sri Lanka

Preface

Celebrating the Unsung

Community radio is an unsung hero among the fourth estate: media. Although a less-talked-about medium, it is the most powerful tool for reaching out to people at the last mile. For more than two decades, community radio as a movement and a necessity for democracies has been discussed globally. While community radio differs from continent to continent, one of the earliest countries to create a national policy in this regard was India. As one of the authors of this book, Dr. Sreedher was fortunate to have launched the first licensed community radio in India in an education institute under the policy on February 1, 2004. For the past fourteen years, the movement has come a long way. As of December, 2018, the number of community radio stations in India is 250.

Even though the community radio sector has covered many milestones along its journey, it still grapples with several challenges; one of the major hurdles in the growth of the sector is sustainability of community radios. The lack of availability of professionally trained community radio broadcasters is one sustainability factor, others being financial and technical sustainability and content development. However, despite these challenges and the lack of attention to the sector, community radios have bridged the information divide in media dark areas, stood as an information lifeline for areas struck with disaster, and acted as a catalyst for increased transparency in our governance system. There is much power in these two words joined together: community and radio. Role of community and participatory content development is the key to community radio. As community radio stations in many areas have embarked on a journey to revive the local folk and fading art forms, it has become an effective means to preserve our cultural heritage.

India has got more than a thousand recognized institutions offering various forms of courses in journalism and mass communication, and electronic media, but there is not much written about community radio in the entire syllabus; which limits the learning and adoption of the medium further. There are very few books like the UNESCO *Handbook of Community Radio* published in early 2000,or books like *Other Voices* by Vinod Pavarala and Kanchan Malik available for practitioners and students to learn about community radio. In 2008, Indira Gandhi National Open University in association with the Commonwealth Educational Media Centre for Asia launched a certificate course in community radio. The material had contributions from people associated with the movement including the UNESCO. It was specially written for students studying through the distant mode. Given this context, there is hardly any systematic way for community radio applicants to get training to run the community radio well, to broadcast content, and to be able to sustain all this. In order to meet the need for a comprehensive textbook on community radio, bringing together the academic and practitioners' perspectives, this book shares the complete process to set up a community radio station, along with the latest guidelines, methods to sustain the radio, and content development through participatory approach. Al Amin, communication advisor, South Asia, UNESCO, encouraged the authors to come out with an updated book and came forward to write the foreword under the seal of UNESCO.

The authors express their thanks to Mr. K.K. Saxena of Aakar Books who agreed to publish this book in a very short period. It is hoped that this book satisfies the needs of all communication students in India and other developing nations and more and more trained knowledgeable human resources available to the community radio sector.

R. Sreedher
Pooja O. Murada

1

A History of Airwaves and the Evolution of Radio

Introduction

This chapter describes the evolution of radio, the first experiments with sound waves at the global level, and their transcendence to the whole world. Particular focus here is on India's radio history and the developments that took place in public, commercial, and community radio. This lays the foundation of the other chapters by offering a chronology of community radio development in India that highlights commonalities and differences in radio movements in different parts of the world.

Chapter Structure
❍ History of Airwaves
❍ Global Scenario
❍ Indian Scenario

History of Airwaves

The idea for radio germinated in Britain by James Maxwell in 1865. Scientist Maxwell's mathematical theory lead to the concept of "electromagnetic waves", a form of energy that passes through the air. Though James Maxwell and other scientists were not able to prove the theory, an experiment by German scientist Heinrich Hertz in 1887 that proved that electromagnetic waves, or energy, passed through the air from one device to another. Radio waves became known as Hertzian waves.

Italian physicist Guglielmo Marconi brought further improvements to a device created for the passage of Hertzian waves in a project he started working on in Italy in 1894. Marconi was soon able to transmit sound across a distance of several kilometers. In 1897, he established the Wireless Telegraph and Signal Company. The company opened the world's first radio factory in Chelmsford, England, in 1898 *(guglielmo-marconi).

The first commercial radio broadcast was transmitted from Pittsburgh, Pennsylvania, on radio station KDKA on the evening of November 2, 1920. Announcers shared the results of the presidential election. The advent of radio as a popular medium brought drastic changes in the thought processes of listeners. Millions of people across the country were able to hear news about important events and political candidates, as well as listen to music.

Modern forms of communications technology, including television broadcasts, satellites, cellphones, radio-controlled toys, and much more, can all be attributed to the early work of British scientist James Maxwell and German scientist Heinrich Hertz.

The Bombay Presidency Radio Club and other radio clubs initiated broadcasting in India in July 1923. The private Indian Broadcasting Company Ltd signed an agreement to operate two radio stations; the first station, in Bombay, began on July 23, 1927, followed by the Calcutta station on August 26, 1927. However, on March 1, 1930, the private company got dissolved and shut down. Subsequently, the government took over the broadcasting facilities as a two-year pilot program, beginning the Indian State Broadcasting Service (ISBS) on April 1, 1930. The decision to continue with the project permanently was made in May 1932. On June 8, 1936, the ISBS was renamed All India Radio (AIR). Simultaneously, the Madras Radio Club was established at Egmore in 1927.

In 1946, AIR was transferred to the Department of Information and Broadcasting. In 1947, independent India, the AIR network, had only six stations: Delhi, Bombay (now Mumbai), Calcutta (now Kolkata), Madras (now Chennai), Lucknow, and Tiruchirappalli. Three radio stations, in Lahore, Peshawar, and Karachi, went to Pakistan after Partition. The total number of radio sets in India at that time was about 275,000.

The Vividh Bharati Service was launched on October 3, 1957. On November 23, 1997, Prasar Bharati (Broadcasting Corporation of India), an autonomous statutory body, was constituted under the Prasar Bharati Act (1990) and came into existence in 1998. Gyan Vani, an educational FM radio station, was launched in several cities of India.

In March 2000, the Ministry of Human Resource Development auctioned radio licenses and assigned a frequency for educational broadcasting in each of forty cities. The Ministry handed the task to India Gandhi National Open University (IGNOU) as it already had some experience telecasting educational programs on Gyan Darshan. One of the authors of this book Dr Sreedher was the Director of Electronic Media Production Centre at IGNOU . In order to reduce the cost and time , IGNOU signed a memorandum of understanding (MOU) with Prasar Bharati that Prasar Bharati would provide the infrastructure and set up and operate the FM stations for educational broadcasts in Allahabad, Bangalore, Bhopal, Coimbatore, Lucknow, and Visakhapatnam. GyanVani's Educational FM Radio Network spread to thirty-seven cities and towns across the country. For years, Gyan Vani struggled to sustain itself and then closed down. The government made efforts to start it again in 2016. It has since been revived and has been on AIR since the later part of 2017 and is re-energizing the channels in a slow and steady manner.

In India, FM broadcasting began in 1977 in Chennai and later expanded in the 1980s. During the mid-nineties, private players obtained FM slots in Delhi, Kolkata, Chennai, Mumbai, and Goa, followed by stations in Bangalore, Hyderabad, Jaipur, and Lucknow. During Phase I in 1999, the government announced a liberalized policy for the expansion of FM radio broadcasting through private agencies and allowing fully owned Indian companies to set up private FM radio stations on a license fee basis. This policy expanded FM broadcasting through private agencies. This policy provided a Grant of Permission based on a one-time entry fee and annual fees as revenue sharing in contrast with the earlier fixed annual license fee regime*(pib.nic.in).

Phase III auctions have sought to expand the availability of FM radio channels in Indian cities previously not covered under the Phase-I and Phase-II auctions and likely to fetch the government more than Rs 1,000 crore as a one-time entry fee from private players in the FM radio industry. This demonstrated that FM radio companies were willing to incur significant expenditure to expand their networks.

The Emergence of Community Media

In an age of development and growth, it is imperative to make the bottom of the pyramid part of this story. In a country as vast and diverse as India, achieving this inclusion is difficult. As is often said, there are two India's within the same country, and it is important to take measures and action to bridge the ever-increasing gap. The basic building block for achieving the same is to spread information and create awareness. A step in this direction is community media . Let us look at how forces, global and local, shaped the domain of community media.

Wikipedia defines Community media as any form of media that function in service of or by a community. It is the rise of all kinds of alternative, oppositional, participatory and collaborative media practices that have developed in the journalistic context of 'community media,' 'we media,' 'citizens media,' 'grassroot journalism' or any radical alternative to on and offline mainstream journalistic practices. In other words, it is having access to or creating local alternatives to mainstream broadcasting, like local community newspapers, radio stations, or magazines. Community Media aids in the process of building citizenship and raising social awareness. "Participation" and "access" are a large aspect in the rise of community media. Those who create media are being encouraged to involve themselves in providing a platform for others to express views. Community media is often given parameters when being defined by groups, but often challenges these boundaries with its broad yet narrow structure. (https://en.wikipedia.org/wiki/Community_radio)

Forms of Community Media

Community media can be print, radio, television, web-based or mixed media.

In 1968 the first Public-access television station in the United States considered to be community media was set up in Dale City, Virginia. It was broadcasting programming for two years without advertising. It was closed down due to lack of financing, equipment, and infrastructure.[Another example of community media is found in the counterculture video collectives of the 1960s and 1970s. The community media expression in Europe began in the 1970s after North American Public-access television was underway. It was therefore seen as a model but also understood that the media environments were structurally different. A powerful community media example is the Bolivian Miners' Radio of the 1940s. Local miner's union launched the station and became an important tool for communication, resistance, and educational and cultural expression.

UNESCO released the Community Media Sustainability Policy Series to help community broadcasters overcome the obstacles they face. UNESCO came out with the following recommendations put forward by stakeholders and participants at an international seminar for Community Media Sustainability: Strengthening Policies and Funding event held by UNESCO in 2015 to promote a healthy policy environment:

Definition of community broadcasting: Community broadcasters should be defined by their independent nature, community governance and focus on issues of local concern.

Formal recognition: Community broadcasters should be considered separate from private and state media in a country's laws and given the same protection afforded to other media.

Licensing: A country should ensure that licensing procedures are fair and transparent, as well as less demanding than the process for commercial media.

Spectrum: a minimum percentage of the broadcasting spectrum should be reserved for community media use.

Provision of public funding: countries should ensure that a continued source of funding is provided for community broadcasters to apply for to increase their sustainability.

Access to Private Funding and Support: Community broadcasters should be allowed the right to utilize private sources of funding, such as income through advertising.

Digital provisions: countries should ensure that community media can access and afford opportunities in the digital space.* (source: UNESCO).

Global Scenario

Community Radio is particularly widespread around the world.

Present-day community radio (CR) has germinated from the pioneering experiences in Latin America some sixty years ago. This has been due mainly to the widespread liberalization of the airwaves, technological growth; diminishing costs of the technology, and a takeout for alternatives to government-controlled and commercial media. The Miners' Radio in Bolivia (1947) and the Peasants' Radio in Colombia (1952) were the predecessors of contemporary community radio. Poverty and social inequity served as the stimulant for these experiences. Community radio is the premier medium of the poor because it jumps the roadblock of isolation and illiteracy, and it is the most affordable electronic medium of communication for the poor and marginalized.

Another model is the network of radio stations, the National Public Radio (NPR) in the USA. NPR is a nonprofit membership based media organization in America. It is a coalition with around 1000 public radio stations in the United States. With support from the international organisations like

UNESCO and others; community radios has received an uplift in the number and popularity in the last two decades.

In Europe, community radio became a vital phenomenon as an alternative to mainstream media in the late '60s and '70s, causing the national broadcasting systems to introduce legitimate community radio. In the '70s and '80s, plagiarizing of radio stations arose in different parts of the UK, run by persons from the West Indies in Manchester, Birmingham, and Bristol. The launch of Lumbini in Philippines by the late Louie Tabing opened the community radio airwaves as did the Radio Kothmale project in Sri Lanka in the late '80s in which Wijayananda Jayaweera played a major role.

Community radio in Africa started in 1982 in Kenya. Between the year 2000 to 2006, the growth of community radio was larger than commercial radios throughout Africa. As compare to the 360 per cent growth of commercial radio, the community radios rose by a prominent 1,386 per cent, on average, over the same period. The Democratic Republic of Congo (DRC) has about 250 community radio stations, whereas they only had ten in the year 2000. In Mali, community radio grew at a rate of two new stations per month throughout the 1990s. In 1997 Nepal had only one community radio (the pioneering Radio Sagarmatha); but now, around 70 per cent of the population is within reach of one of twenty-two community-managed radio stations.

In Colombia, since broadcasting liberalization in the 1990s, the number of community stations has risen to around 850. Total radio stations by country range from three or four in countries such as Rwanda and Kenya, to South Africa with ninety-two community stations, Mali with 159, and the DRC with more than 250. Smaller countries such as Liberia have about thirty-four active community radio stations; and Sierra Leone, with twenty-four, has seen particularly large increases in recent years.

After the 1990s, community radio burgeoned in Africa and worldwide. Some countries, such as Eritrea and Zimbabwe, banned community radio completely, while more liberal governments, as in Mali and South Africa, embraced it.

Since the 1990s, community radio has mushroomed across the developing world, in fact, growing faster than either state or commercial radio. Recent years have seen a substantial trend toward the legitimization and initiation of new community radio stations as well as expansion of the media.

In South Asia, India introduced community radio legislation as recently as 2002 and thus opened the way for bringing 1.2 billion more of the world's population into the orbit of community radio. Bangladesh and Afghanistan are slowly becoming more interested in establishing community radio. Bangladesh introduced community media legislation in 2008; and in Afghanistan, there are about thirty-five community-owned radio stations in a difficult but increasingly less-controlled press environment. However, in Pakistan, the Pakistan Electronic Media Regulatory Authority (PEMRA) rules are clear on allowing community-based radio stations, but not a single license is granted so far. Bhutan currently prohibits nonprofit-based community stations with the monopoly under the Bhutan Broadcasting Services (BBS); and in Sri Lanka the national broadcasting corporation, the Sri Lanka Broadcasting Corporation (SLBC), controls many local stations with some community radio characteristics, but they are rarely critical of the government.

In Southeast Asia, Thailand tops the region's graph with about 5,000 community-owned stations, but most of them are operating without licenses. In populous Indonesia, community radio has also taken off rapidly, but the number of stations is in the hundreds. In the Philippines, more than fifty-five community radio stations independent of government and commercial interests are functioning outside the cities and practicing with low-quality transmitters. Elsewhere, the regimes in Laos, Burma, Malaysia, and Vietnam are moving toward bottling up community media in varying degrees. By contrast, Cambodia's media setting is relatively free but has only a handful of internationally endorsed community radios.

Colombia, Bolivia, Mexico, and Argentina have specialized friendly pro-community broadcasting policies. The total number of community radio stations in Latin America is around 10,000, with Peru having the prominent proportion and Ecuador, Bolivia, and Brazil in second, third, and fourth place. If unlicensed stations are also taken into consideration, then the overall numbers are more eminent. But a new challenge has emerged: the sustainability of community radio with ensuring a high-level of community participation. (Source: UNESCO.org)

Indian Scenario

Discussions about community radio broadcasting in India began in the 1960s with a series of reports, meetings, and proposals aimed at achieving the legal recognition of community-based radio stations and the abolition of the government monopoly over the media. When referring to inclusive development, some instruments are needed that will act as catalysts for bringing the change. The fairly new concept of narrowcasting is predicted to emerge as an effective alternative to mainstream media. Community radio is envisaged as one such alternative.

Milestones in the process include the Chanda Committee Report 1966, which initiated the debate to end the monopoly of All India Radio (AIR). This subsequently led to an historic ruling in 1995 by the Supreme Court Jurisdiction calling upon the government, inter alia, to draw up regulations for granting licenses to private broadcasters and for the establishment of an autonomous and independent authority responsible for supervising all the operational aspects of broadcasting. These rulings shift from a state broadcasting system to a highly commercial system.

In 1996, representatives from universities, AIR, non-governmental organizations, and other sectors of society met in Bangalore and drew up the declaration "Towards public service broadcasting through community radio." Four years later in 2000, a group of media professionals, researchers, educators, representatives from AIR, and radio enthusiasts drafted an outline of community radio broadcasting policy, which they called the "Pastapur Initiative on Community Radio Broadcasting." The document urged the government to recognize the community broadcasting service as a third kind of service, distinct from public and commercial broadcasting, and to allocate frequencies for creation, expansion, and maintenance of the service. Furthermore, in the view of socioeconomic disparities, the group recommended that priority be given to rural areas and less-developed regions to get licenses for establishing community radio stations.

The government of the day did not find it appropriate to grant licenses for community radio and instead offered radio frequencies for education. During the first phase of FM wave auctions, one frequency was reserved for education in all the forty cities where the spectrum was allotted. The responsibility of running these stations fell upon IGNOU, which, as a nodal agency, launched the Gyan Vani radio stations. These stations had the same power as commercial radio stations and broadcast from the same tower. IGNOU signed the agreement with Prasar Bharati whose CEO and the present Lieutenant Governor of Delhi, Mr. Anil Baijal, to collocate their transmitters and antenna on AIR or Doordarshan towers. The same was replicated with other commercial stations. IGNOU formed an expert committee, which included activists interested in community radio for Gyan Vani and offered 40 per cent of the broadcast time to community broadcasts. But there was lukewarm response, and neither side took any major steps to implement the suggestions.

In 2003 when IGNOU was simultaneously launching four radio stations (in Lucknow, Coimbatore, Mumbai, and Visakhapatnam), the ministers, Sushma Swaraj and Dr Murli Manohar Joshi, were impressed by the potential of these stations and decided to allow the community radio station to educational institutions in the first instance . The CR policy 2002 was announced in early 2003, and fifty-seven institutions applied that year. However, the procedure was elaborate, including a clearance by the state government.

Anna CR is India's first campus community radio that was launched on February 1, 2004, hosted by Educational Multimedia Research Centre. The co-author, Dr. R. Sreedher, had the opportunity of giving shape to Gyan Vani as well as to the first community radio station in India. Being the first CR station, it had grappled with many challenges. Nevertheless, the importance of the medium was established and the government decided to replicate the community radio model to other states too.

Anna University in association with the Commonwealth of Learning organized an international conference on community radio, which had representation from thirteen countries including Pakistan. Fifty-five applicants were trained over two weeks by international trainers such as the late Louie Tabing, M.J.R. David from Sri Lanka, and BBC correspondent David Walker from the Commonwealth of Learning, Canada. The government took keen interest in the outcome and recommendations of the workshop. Some of the recommendations included that the community radio sector should be expanded to the civil society and NGO sector, and five minutes of advertisement per hour should be permitted along with simplification of the licensing process including the suggestion of having a single window for application.

When a tsunami struck the coast of Chennai on December 26, 2004, Mr. Naveen Chawla, then Secretary at the Ministry of Information and Broadcasting, was in Chennai. He happened to witness the functioning of a community radio during a natural disaster and got convinced of the utility of the media at the local levels. He set the ball rolling and a group of ministers were appointed by the government, headed by Mr. Sharad Pawar (Minister of Agriculture), Mr. P. Chidambaram (Minister of Finance), and Mr. Dayanidhi Maran (Minister of Telecom) to relook and revise the community radio policy. Meanwhile, a community radio, *Vasundhara Vahini* was established in his constituency Baramati in Maharashtra state . Hence the chairperson of GOM had firsthand knowledge and experience working in grassroots community radio.

On November 16, 2006, the government of India released a revised CR policy with a new set of Community Radio Guidelines that allowed NGOs and other civil society organizations, Krishi Vigyan Kendras, and agriculture universities to possess and operate community radio stations.

Since the Indian broadcasting media is undergoing a transition from government monopoly to a highly commercialized broadcasting network, citizens are also demanding democratization of media. One can easily appreciate the need for community radio in India, a country with more than twenty officially recognized languages and more than 1,500 dialects. Community radio holds the key potential to unite India's linguistic and ethnic diversity, improve the economic diversity, and fill the huge urban-rural divide.

When Sangham Radio in Pastapur village, Medak district, Andhra Pradesh, went on air on October 15, 2008, it was the first community-based radio station as distinct from a campus-based radio in India. Sangham Radio 90.4 MHz is hosted by the Deccan Development Society (DDS), an NGO that works with women's groups in Andhra Pradesh. A second community radio, *Radio Bundelkhand*, was launched on October 23, 2008, and based in Orchha, Madhya Pradesh. The Society for Development Alternatives (DA), a Delhi-based NGO, is the license holder for Radio Bundelkhand.

Over the past six years, community-based programming has taken root in different parts of India, with the purpose to empower communities through access to information and communication skills. According to government sources, the vision was to have more than 4,000 community radios across India by 2008, but the statistics from 2017 show that India is still far away from the set target.

By December 2018, as per the Government of India, Ministry of Information and Broadcasting (MIB), the total number of permission holders for establishing community radio is 250, and the letter of intent (LOI) holders number 562 across the country. Of 206 stations operated in 2012, 112 were educational, seventy-nine were NGOs, and fifteen were KVK/SAU.

The different era of radio in India in chronological order illustrates the development of radio:

I. Age of Formulation

1885 : Indian Telegraph Act

1923 : Cinematography Act

1941 : Department of Information and Broadcasting set up.

II. Age of Consolidation

1951 : The Indian Telegraph Act (1895) extended to the whole of India.

1952 : The Cinematograph Act amended to extend to the whole of India.

1966 : Ashok K. Chanda Committee Report on Broadcasting and Information Media

"It is not possible in the Indian context for a creative medium like broadcasting to flourish under a regiment (sic) of departmental rules and regulations. It is only by an institutional change that AIR can be liberated from present rigid financial and administrative procedures of Government."

1978 : Akash Bharti Bill

"The Govt. has decided not to set up an autonomous body of AIR and Doordarshan as recommended by the Verghese Group because such an organization is not considered necessary to enable those mass media to discharge their basic objective of serving the people who are not served by other media."

1982 : Parthasarathy committee on Working Group on Software for Doordarshan

"The freedom of the communicator to produce must be harmonized with the right of the weaker sections constituting the vast majority in a developing country to be truly represented in software. The over-representation of the elite and the negligible representation or false representation of the weak in software is an issue which is as serious and fundamental as the issue of creative freedom."

III. Age of Uncertainty

1995 : Supreme Court Judgement by P.B. Sawant, S. Mohan, and B.P. Jeevan Reddy (Ministry of Information and Broadcasting, Govt. of India vs. Cricket Association of Bengal)

"It is also urged that there is no exclusive privilege or monopoly in relation to production, transmission, or telecasting and such an exclusive monopoly, if claimed, is violative of Article 19(1) (a)."

"There is no doubt that since the airwaves/frequencies are a public property and are also limited, they have to be used in the best interest of the society and this can be done either by a central authority by establishing its own broadcasting network or regulating the grant of licenses to other agencies including the private agencies."

1996 : National Media Policy

"Adequate care should be taken to enable the setting up of non-commercial broadcasting stations to be run by universities, educational institutions, panchayats/local bodies, State Governments, etc."

"A new production style, which is people-oriented should be developed. In tune with the policy framework suggested here, the Indian private sector/State Government/NGOs/Local Government should be allowed to enter the field of broadcasting/telecasting."

"The apex regulatory body should be an independent autonomous public authority representative of all sections and interests in the society and should control and regulate the use of air waves in the interests of the public and to prevent invasion of their rights encouraged."

1996 : Constitution of High Power Committee for the Implementation of the Prasar Bharati Act

"Recommended that the local terrestrial TV and radio stations should be permitted. These stations will also help municipal bodies and panchayati raj institutions in providing local broadcasting services to the community. For this purpose, the Indian Telegraph Act, 1885, could be suitably amended."

IV. Age of Accountability and Liberalization

2002 : Policy Guidelines for Setting Community Radio Stations (for setting up of community radio stations to well-established educational institutions including IITs/IIMs.)

2004 : First community radio situated at Anna University campus was launched.

2004 : UNESCO organises the First National Consultation for Community Radio at Delhi.

2004 : First meeting of all applicants for Community radio at Anna University Chennai as part of the International workshop on Community Radio.

2005 : Department of Science and Technology supported *Science for women's health and nutrition* radio project in Anna University as a pilot.

2006 : New Policy Guidelines for Setting Community Radio Station (Government decided to broadbase the policy by bringing nonprofit organizations like civil society and voluntary organizations, under its ambit.)

2007 : A membership body of community radios called Community Radio Forum launched.

2007 : Community Radio Awareness campaigns were initiated as a part of information education and communications (IEC) activities by the Ministry of Information and

Broadcasting (MIB). Commonwealth Educational Media Centre for Asia (CEMCA) was given the charge to hold these workshops for next five years. During the year 2007–08, two regional-level consultations were organized at Uttar Pradesh and West Bengal. Six regional-level consultations were held at Puducherry, Maharashtra, Gujarat, Assam, Himachal Pradesh, and Chhattisgarh. During 2009–10, ten state-level consultations took place at Rajasthan, Meghalaya, Haryana, Madhya Pradesh, Tamil Nadu, Kerala, Karnataka, Maharashtra, Uttarakhand, and Uttar Pradesh. In 2010–11, efforts were made to connect with unreached states such as Andhra Pradesh, Punjab, Tripura, Odisha, Jammu & Kashmir, and Andaman & Nicobar. As a result, four regional-level consultations took place at Andhra Pradesh, Punjab, Agartala, and Odisha.

2007 : MIB and UNESCO organises National Consultation on Community Radio for practising and potential Community Radio Operators in India', at the Indian Institute of Mass Communication (IIMC), New Delhi, 6-7 March.

2008 : First meeting of the heads of functional community radio stations at Anna University organised on behalf of the Ministry of Information and Broadcasting (MIB).

2009 : Directorate of Advertising and Visual Publicity (DAVP) announced one rupee per second as the rates for advertisement for Community Radio stations.

2010 : MIB and UNESCO organises the second National Consultation on Community Radio at Delhi.

2011 : MIB organised first CR sammelan at New Delhi and release of the compendium of community radios in India. CEMCA initiates awards for Community Radio Stations.

2011 : Idea of a membership body called *Community Radio Association* mooted and later got registered.

2011 : DAVP rates revised to rupee four per second.

2011 : Community Radio Facilitation Centre launched at Shastri Bhawan and in CEMCA using a bilateral agency grant.

2012 : Second CR Sammelan at New Delhi - Government of India took over the CR awards and made it a National award with cash incentives.

2013 : Federation of Community radio stations formed.

2017 : UNESCO Chair on community media organises National Consultation on Community Radio in India.

2017 : Government of India enhances the subsidy for Community Radio station to 90 per cent in north eastern states and for others to 75 per cent. Support for creation of content also announced in the guidelines.

2018 : Government announces easing of regulations to the Government owned educational institutions and Krishi Vigyan Kendras. Also the restriction on educational institutions to locate the transmitter within their main campus is withdrawn. The condition that one institution will be offered only one frequency is also withdrawn in the case of Government run institutions. For non government organisations the applications and the geo-coordinates have to be routed through the district administration.

2019 : The number of community radio awareness workshops, regional sammelans and sammelans is nearing a century.

Key Terms

Community radio. A medium to spread information and create awareness by and for community.

Gyan Vani. A network of educational FM radio stations in India under the Ministry of Human Resource Development.

NPR. (National Public Radio) A privately and publicly funded nonprofit membership media organization in America that serves as a national syndicator to a network of 900 public radio stations in the United States.

NGOs. Non-governmental organizations

KVK. Krishi Vigyan Kendras

SAU. State Agriculture Universities

IEC. Information Education and Communications

Chanda Committee Report 1966. A report that initiated a debate to end the monopoly of All of India Radio.

2

Community Radio Through a Governance Lens

Introduction

This chapter highlights the interplay of various governance processes including decision-making structures and implementation processes associated with community radio; explores the importance of community participation in the form of advisory and management committees to strengthen the operations of a community radio station and ensure sustainability of people and content; and examines the licensing processes and the checks and balances put in place for community broadcasting.

Chapter Structure

- Governance and Community Radio
- Advisory and Management Committees
- Ensuring Transparency

"When radio fosters the participation of citizens and defends their interests; when it reflects the tastes of the majority and makes good humour and hope its main purpose; when it truly informs; when it helps resolve the thousand and one problems of daily life; when all ideas are debated in its programs and all opinions are respected; when cultural diversity is stimulated over commercial homogeneity; when women are main players in communication and not simply a pretty voice or a publicity gimmick; when no type of dictatorship is tolerated, not even the musical dictatorship of the big recording studios; when everyone's words fly without discrimination or censorship, that is community radio. Of course this service is highly political: it is a question of influencing public opinion, denying conformity, creating consensus, broadening democracy. The purpose—whence the name—is to build community life.'' José Ignacio Lopez Vigil. 1997

"As media, they develop pluralistic and participatory communication that is open to the need for expression of the social and cultural sectors with less access to exclusively commercial media. That exercise the right to communication and, particularly, the right to information. That exercise radio broadcasting as a service, and not simply as a commercially profitable activity.'' Federación Argentina de Radios Comunitarias, FARCO. Argentina.

''Free, independent, lay radio stations that are linked to human rights and concerned about the environment. They are many and pluralistic. They refuse mercantile communication. They scrupulously respect the code of ethics of journalists and work to disseminate culture by giving artists broader expression within their listening audiences. They have association status, democratic operation and financing consistent with the fact that they are non-profit organizations. They are solidarity toward each other and constitute work communities that make it possible for each member to fulfill its mission to the utmost.'' Charte de la Confédération Nationale des Radios Libres, CNRL, France.

With such distinct characteristics of a unique medium having the potential to build community life, the approach to governance also has to be unique—the way community radio governs itself and its operations, weaving community participation at every step in multiple ways.

Governance and Community Radio

Governance, as the word suggests, refers to the decision-making structures and implementation processes, in this case at a community radio station. These structures and processes are expected to be transparent and participatory in nature. Why is this necessary? The answer is simple: the primary objective of a CR station is to hold paramount the interests of the targeted community. Besides this, it is important that the marginalized and poor communities in the broadcast area, who may live in media-dark areas or have limited access to information platforms, have a say and role in this important medium of communication.

In addition to the above, the license-holder organization should have a sound understanding of the community within the broadcast reach and engage the excluded communities in the radio by empowering them to take decisions on behalf of and as a community. Apart from this, being vocal about problems, jointly finding solutions, and participating in the generation of content are also significant aspects that call for contributions from the community.

In the governance of a community radio station, two separate committees are necessary. One is the apex committee constituted by the licensing organization. This body takes care of the licensing process, annual maintenance of equipment, staff structure, budget, auditing, submission of necessary documents to the government and other statutory bodies, grievances, protection of women and minorities, and legal aspects, etc. Apart from the authority and responsibilities, crisis management also falls under the purview of the authorized signatory of the committee. The authorized signatory can be sued if there is any breach of broadcasting code of ethics. One can sue on behalf of the station. For example, in most universities, the registrar might be sued. In many cases, it is the secretary or secretary general or the convener who will be sued. In the CR scenario, the authorized signatory for obtaining the licenses should be the authority to be sued or to sue on behalf of the station.

The second required committee is the content management committee, which consists mainly of people in and around the listening zone. The number of members can be as few as

15 per cent from the parent organization, which will include the station manager as the convenor.

Studying the research and data available from the area, organizing focus group meetings, understanding the local needs, and preparation of long-term and short-term program content are the main functions of this body. This committee takes responsibility for broadcast contents while the legal responsibility of broadcasting lies with the first committee. This committee also serves as an ethics committee. It should ensure maximum participation of the community where the signals reach as well as decide the types of coverage, advertisements, etc., and see that the vested interests do not take control of the contents with financial support or the use of political or muscle power.

Advisory and Management Committees

Why is an advisory body important? It's not just about advice, it's also content management.

An advisory body consists of members who represent different sections of the community in the broadcast area. The role of an advisory body pertains to the operations of a community radio station. The body provides directions regarding programming, a task which is important in making the content relevant and interesting. This makes the body instrumental in preparing a broadcast policy. Members of this body may also act as local ambassadors for the radio station. Regular meetings of the advisory body are necessary, as dynamic challenges faced by the station can be addressed and curtailed in a timely manner. The minimum number of members this "community radio content management committee" should have is either: eleven, thirteen, or fifteen. They may represent the majority or minority religion, majority or minority linguistic group, caste, or communities. Care must be taken to give equal representation to women. The whole committee should appear balanced, i.e. include members from Hindu, Christian, Muslim, Sikh, Jain, and Buddhist, oppressed and depressed classes, various age groups and economic strata. Care must be taken to include a majority of persons from economically weaker sections. An anthropologist, a social scientist, and a statistician may be engaged to give advice on the composition of the committee.

Steps in forming the advisory/content committee for a community radio station:

1. Selection of places/villages, area map and randomization of the villages, and rotation of the samples at predetermined durations; with the help of a statistician and social scientist.
2. Visit the places and talk to peer leaders and common citizens.
3. Identify names suitable for the committee.
4. Explain the community radio concept and play program excerpts. Ensure that the members are reasonably aware of the community radio concept. An orientation and a visit to CR stations are needed before finalizing the members.
5. Answer their questions.
6. Survey 500 people from the coverage area regarding their needs, available media, media gap, and local talent.
7. Make sure that listening facilities such as radio receivers and earphones are available, and that the radio signal reaches the coverage area. On visits, carry some radio sets, and play some programs through the transmitter.
8. Form the committee and call for a meeting.
9. The terms of reference (TOR) for the committee should be given to them prior the first meeting so they can study/ listen to them and give their acceptance.

Sample Points for the Terms of Reference

a. Plan the survey and identify volunteers and the strategy.
b. Supervise the survey and conduct random checks.
c. Analyze survey results conducted from time to time from the community and focus on subjects and topics to be broadcast for the next three months.

d. Receive reports of the feedback (telephonic, electronic. and postal) from station management.
e. Define the vision and mission statements for the station.
f. Prepare a three-month program statement at the meeting with a template and have it signed by each member. This quarterly schedule for the station will take into account the ground realities, climate, festivals, and pressing demands.
g. Oversee the preparation of a monthly layout for radio programs wherein proper time slots, experts, and participants are identified. In order to ensure a balanced approach, focus should be given on equal participation, avoiding favoritism, and also check the frequent projection of certain individuals and groups..
h. Discuss the number of broadcast hours per day and broad formats and timing at the committee meetings.
i. Identify local festivals, events, and camps, and their prominence will be discussed on the air.
j. Ensure representation from local schools, NGOs, and industrial workers.
k. Document minutes of the meetings.
l. Pay a nominal sum (say Rs. 100 to 500 or any amount that may seem reasonable) as an honorarium per sitting.
m. Meet once in three months on fixed days. Extraordinary meetings of the committee may be held if at least one third of the members participate.
n. Initiate new members every two years. The term of the committee members will be two years
o. Only two members from the parent organization can serve on the committee: its head or his/her nominee, and the station manager.

Management Committee: Management and Beyond

The management committee is the decision-making body for the CRS. It handles the radio setup, administrative and functional matters like budgets, day-to-day programming, formulation of policies, technology, human resources, etc. The management committee comprises of members from the parent organization, staff, volunteers and media experts. The management committee should meet every quarter in order to take an update on the everyday functioning, thereby finding and addressing challenges and serving as advisors to the CR team.

It is important that the staff, advisory body, and management committee are in sync with each other working with a common vision of including the excluded community in the programming to enable the CRS to run in participation with the local community.

Hiring of Staff and Volunteers: Indigenous is the Best Choice

Community radio is by and for the community, so the staff should belong to the community and hiring should be transparent and participatory. Local talent can be identified to perform the tasks for which they are best suited. The management committee will support the staff by having regular trainings in the field of program production and CR management.

Doors should be kept open for volunteers, who can walk into the station and contribute their skills.

Community radio must follow the good labor practices it preaches about. Even if one staff member is appointed, that person has to be covered by a written agreement. Punctuality, discipline, gender sensitivity, compensation, exit policy, and tolerance are all to be specified in the agreement. Staff members must be given reasonable decision-making opportunities including finance. Grievance redressal and various levels of problem-solving must be specified in the understanding. Digital payments, deduction of tax at source, health benefits like group family insurance, life insurance, and incentives to family members for education should also be part of the agreement. Hiring and firing of workers without proper written notice is to be discouraged.

Vision and Mission: The Way Ahead

Vision and mission statements serve as foundational guides in the establishment of a community radio station. At the inception of a CR station, founding members should define its mission, which is a statement defining purpose and objectives that is formulated to ensure that everybody involved has the same understanding and to provide a basis for the station's development. These are also helpful tools in making decisions on programming, governance, and other issues. A mission statement shouldn't be long (two or three sentences suffice), but it should be as specific as possible without dictating daily activities or an exact programming mix.

The management and founders of a community radio station should have ambitious plans for the project. Right at the inception stage or immediately after registration, the founders, as an interim board, should define what the station will be known for and where they aspire to take it. They should have a vision for the community radio station as well. **A vision statement describes what the Radio station desires to achieve in the long-run, generally in a time frame of five to ten years, or sometimes even longer. It depicts a vision of what the station will look like in the future.**

In the case of the *Alfaz-e-Mewat* community radio station, which is operating for marginalized communities in the rural area of Nuh district, Haryana, India, the vision and mission statements evolved over time. These statements are in the thoughts of the radio station team and reflect in their day-to-day actions.

Vision and mission statements should not be cast in stone, but be reviewed periodically and adjusted with changing times, for which a periodical review is vital

Vision and mission statements documented by CRS Alfaz-E-Mewat FM 107.8 Vision

Alfaz-e-Mewat envisions working together with and for all sections of rural communities to bridge the information divide, provide citizens with a platform to share, create awareness, disseminate information on agriculture, water, soil health, enable good rural governance, and be a source of edutainment.

Mission

- To be a successful and sustainable community-led public private partnership model
- To disseminate information that is directly relevant to the community
- To use radio as an outreach tool for farming communities to share their voices
- To use radio as a tool to accelerate the rural development process
- To preserve and promote Mewati culture and language
- To disseminate information across various themes in an interactive and entertaining format

Legal Framework of Community Radio

Communication advocates have long argued that communication can contribute to governance by influencing opinions, attitudes, and ultimately the behavior of key stakeholders, including leaders, bureaucrats, and citizens. This is easy to achieve through the medium of community radio.

Guidelines for community radio stations in India were established in 2002. The policy then allowed only educational institutions to set up and operate community radio stations. The first campus community radio station was launched in Anna University at Chennai in 2004. Keeping in mind the developmental challenges of India and the aspirations of people to have a medium which they can call their own, the Ministry of Information and Broadcasting announced a modified policy in 2006 that brought a paradigm shift, as it permitted nonprofit organizations to apply for community radio licenses.

More than eleven-and-a-half years after the Supreme Court of India passed its landmark judgment in 1995, stating that air waves were public property to be used for public good, community-based NGOs became eligible to apply for a license to operate a community radio station of their own. The government liberalized the policy for community radio in December 2006 and decided to grant permissions for setting up CR stations to nonprofit organizations (civil society and voluntary organizations), state agricultural universities, Indian Council of Agricultural Research (ICAR) institutions, Krishi Vigyan Kendras, registered societies and autonomous bodies, and registered public trusts.

What is the role of CR in a community? In a nutshell, CR aims at enhancing participation of community members in the development process and capacity building in rural areas with education. CR provides opportunities for people to upgrade their skills and enhance their creative talents while also preserving and promoting their traditional wisdom, knowledge, and skills. Thereby, CR helps to promote and protect local language, arts, craft, culture, and traditions. CR brings topical information within easy reach of the rural population in areas of agriculture, social welfare, education, health, and the environment and helps to create networks for rural cottage and village industries.

More than 253 operational CR stations are on the air as of November 2018 in different parts of India. And the number is growing. In December 2010, the Ministry of Information and Broadcasting worked out a scheme called Community Radio Sustenance Fund and got it cleared through the Planning commission. Such a move was sought by the National Consultation on Community Radio supported by UNESCO, Community Radio Forum, Commonwealth of Learning, CEMCA, the Ford Foundation etc. Earlier attempts to create a Private Trust to support the CR sector was called off. Later, the Ministry of Information and Broadcasting put together a working group to set up a framework to operationalize the fund. This policy document envisages community radios to broadcast programs on health, education, environment, and community development with total community participation.

The Community Radio National Guidelines (Ministry of Information & Broadcasting, 2006) specifically charge that the CR management structure should be reflective of the community that the station seeks to serve. Through community radio, efforts are also being made to promote dialogic empowerment in rural areas with the help of more than 260,000 gram panchayats and over two million non-governmental organizations in the country. These efforts envisage taking advantage of the public-private partnerships in rural India, between panchayati raj institutions and civil society organizations. The central government has instituted Community Radio Awards and set up a Community Radio Facebook page. The annual CR Convention, supplemented with regional capacity-building workshops in rural areas, is one of many initiatives to further strengthen the CR system.

The statutory basis of government monopoly of the broadcast sector, which was widespread until the emergence of satellite television in the 1990s, can be traced to the 123-year-old Indian Telegraph Act of 1885. According to the Act, the central government has the exclusive privilege of establishing, maintaining, and working telegraphs within India. The Act, and its subsequent amendments, defines telegraph broadly to include most modern communication devices irrespective of their underlying technology.

The Act authorizes the central government to take temporary possession of a telegraph in cases involving public emergencies or public safety. Section 5(2) enables the government to lawfully intercept telegraph messages on reasonable grounds. These include India's sovereignty and integrity, state security, friendly relations with foreign states, public order, and preventing the commission of an offence. The Act empowers the government to revoke a telegraph license for breach of any of the terms and conditions or for a default in making license-fee payments.

Though the Telegraph Act does not explicitly define "telecommunications service" and "broadcasting service," the Telecom Regulatory Authority of India (TRAI) Act, 1997, defines communication service in section 2(1)(k) as: "Service of any description (including electronic mail, voice mail, data services, audio-text services, video-text services, radio paging, and cellular mobile telephones services) which is made available to users by means of a transmission or reception of signals, writing, images, and sounds or intelligence of any nature, by wire, radio, visual, or any other electronic means, but shall not include broadcasting services." (Provided that the central government may notify other services to be telecommunication services including broadcasting services)

Though this section expressly excludes "broadcasting" from this definition, the directive authorizes the government to notify broadcasting services to be a telecommunication service. This notification gave TRAI the authority to regulate broadcasting and cable services in India.

The license required for broadcasting (the Wireless Operating License) is given by the Wireless Planning and Coordination Committee (WPC) Wing of the Ministry of Communication and Information and Technology, while the MIB gives a Grant of Permission Agreement.

Most radio and television services are also regulated by the Indian Wireless Telegraphy Act (No 17 of 1933), as they constitute "wireless communications." Section 2(2) and Section 3 regulate wireless communication by requiring users of various types of wireless equipment to obtain wireless licenses for possessing and using the equipment. These licenses are granted by the WPC (Wireless Planning & Coordination Authority) Wing of the Department of Telecommunications (DoT).

Therefore, to offer most kinds of broadcasting services, a broadcasting company must obtain two types of licenses:

- A Grant of Permission Agreement (GOPA) to offer broadcast services issued by the Ministry of Information and Broadcasting under the Telegraph Act.

- A Wireless Operating License (WOL) from the WPC (Wireless Planning & Coordination Authority) Wing of the Ministry of Communication and Information Technology under the Wireless Telegraphy Act.

Checks and Regulations

All the content being aired by community radio stations must adhere to the All India Radio's Broadcast Code and the Programme Code and Advertisement Code of the Cable Television, Networks (Regulation) Act, 1995. These rules forbid the use of content that criticizes friendly countries, attacks a religion or community, is obscene or derogatory, denigrates women, or incites violence.

The independent media in India object to media regulation. They would prefer self-regulation. All TV channels and news channels created a grievance redressal mechanism by forming the News Broadcast Authority. But the government indirectly monitors TV programs through a centralized mechanism in the form of monitoring center in Delhi. Such a mechanism is not yet in place for community radio stations. The private commercial FM programs are also being monitored by this central facility.

In order to provide a summary on the *Do's and Don'ts* that need to be observed before the setup of a community radio station and during the broadcast of programs, including advertising, a number of supporting documents from different organisations and academic institution is given below.

Broadcasting Code

All India Radio General Broadcasting Code or Programme Code (Already mentioned in the GOPA and CR Policy Guidelines in greater detail), specifies that the CR stations sign an agreement with the Ministry of Information and Broadcasting, Government of India. The General Broadcasting Code, which is otherwise called the Programme Code for both AIR and Doordarshan (the television wing of Prasar Bharati Broadcasting Corporation of India), prohibits criticism of friendly countries, attack on religions or communities, anything obscene or defamatory, inciting violence or against maintenance of law and order, anything amounting to contempt of court, against the integrity of the president and judiciary, and others. (Source: MIB)

Community Radio Ethics (Source: IGNOU)

- A community radio station must broadcast primarily in the language and dialect that the majority of the community speak and understand.
- While describing a person or group, avoid labels such as caste, sect, etc., that may sound offensive.
- Speak in a manner that can be easily followed on radio, **and be cautious or do** not to speak too quickly.
- Keep technical terms to a minimum.
- Achieve maximum participation **from** every section of the community living within the target area.
- Involve the community in ---- planning, research, programming, production, broadcasting, and feedback.
- Reflect the diverse multicultural tastes of the audience in the program policy.
- Apart from entertaining the audience, give them new information, **and** little-known facts, teach them new skills, and bring out their hidden talents.
- Organize training workshops for community members to ensure proper access to the studio and other production facilities.
- Strive to raise the social standard of the target community.

Ethical Conduct of Radio Stations to Ensure Individual/ Institutional Rights and Privacy (National Public Radio Guidelines)

- Plagiarism is an unpardonable offence. When other people's work is broadcast, due credit has to be given to the producer or authority concerned.
- No material from another source should ever be included substantially without attribution. In addition, when a

person gives new information, it is the role of the CR broadcaster to confirm it at least from two reliable sources before airing the information.

- Any story that goes on air must be completely balanced and contain views of both parties.
- No story shall favor a particular caste, religion, political party, etc. This situation might arise easily in a rural community radio setup where the panchayat leader might favor a particular issue and the people might favor another. But it is the duty of the CR broadcaster to properly present the views of both parties on air. Programming is not expected to provide a solution to every problem; the primary duty is to present the issues and problems so the community can find its own solutions.
- Proper permission must be obtained for conducting events or using a public place like a school, park, etc., for recording a special program.
- Every person's individual sentiment must be respected. If a person is not ready to speak on a particular topic, it is better to avoid it.

Code for Commercial Advertising–All India Radio (AIR) 9 A: General Rules of Conduct in Advertising

1. Advertising shall be designed to conform to the laws of the country and should not offend against morality, decency, or religious susceptibilities of the people.
2. No advertisement shall be permitted **to broadcast** that . . .
    - derides any race, caste, color, creed, or nationality.
    - is against any directive principle or any other provision of the Constitution of India.
    - tends to incite people to crime, cause disorder or violence or breach of law, or glorifies violence or obscenity in any way.
    - presents criminality as desirable.
    - adversely affects friendly relations with foreign States.

- exploits the national emblem or any part of the constitution or the person or personality of a national leader or State dignitary.
- relates to or promotes cigarettes and tobacco products (including Pan Masala), alcohol, drugs, or other intoxicants.

3. No advertisement message shall in any way be presented as news.
4. No advertisements shall be permitted where objects are wholly or mainly of a religious or political nature; the advertisement must not be directed toward any religious or political end or be related to any industrial dispute.

   Ethical Practice Guidelines for Community Radio Stations 34 Proviso

   "But advertisements in the form of spots and jingles on payment of prescribed fees, from political parties, candidates, or any other person shall be accepted only in respect of General Elections to Lok Sabha/General Elections to the State Assemblies/General Elections to Local Bodies during the period when the model Code of Conduct is in force. Such advertisements shall be subject to pre-broadcast scrutiny by the Election Commission of India, authorities under the Election Commission of India in respect of elections to Lok Sabha and the State Assemblies and State Election Commissions in the case of Local bodies. "(DG: AIR's I.D. No. 15/3/2008- PIV dated November 20, 2008)"
5. Advertisements for services concerned with the following shall not be accepted:

   Money lenders. • chit funds. • saving schemes and lotteries other than those conducted by central and state government organizations, nationalized or recognized banks and public sector undertakings • matrimonial agencies • unlicensed employment services • fortune tellers or soothsayers, etc., and those with claims of hypnotism • foreign goods or foreign banks • betting tips, guide books, etc., relating to horse racing or the other games of gambling.

6. Items advertised shall not suffer from any defect or deficiency as mentioned in the Consumer Protection Act 1986.
7. No advertisement shall contain reference(s) that are likely to lead the public to infer that the product advertised or any of its ingredients has some special or miraculous or supernatural property or quality that is difficult to be proved, e.g. cure for baldness, skin whitener, etc.
8. No advertisement shall contain the words "guarantee" or "guaranteed," etc., unless the full terms of the guarantee are available for inspection by the directorate general, All India Radio, are clearly set out in the advertisement and are made available to the purchaser in writing at the point of sale or with the goods. In all cases, terms must include details of the remedial action available to the purchaser. No advertisement shall contain a direct or implied reference to any guarantee which purports to take away or diminish the legal rights of the purchaser.
9. Advertisers or the agents must be prepared to produce evidence to substantiate any claims or illustrations. The director general reserves the right to ask for such proofs and have them examined to his full satisfaction. In case of goods covered by mandatory quality control orders, the advertiser shall produce a quality certificate from the institutions recognized by the government for this purpose.
10. Advertisements shall not contain disparaging or derogatory references to another product or service.
11. Testimonials must be genuine and not mislead listeners Advertisers or advertising agencies must be prepared to produce evidence in support of their claims.
12. No advertisement of any kind of jewelry (except artificial jewelry) or precious stones shall be accepted.

13. Advertisements indicating price comparisons or reductions must comply with relevant laws. No advertisement shall be accepted that violates AIR Broadcast Code "Note: Advertisements concerning jewelry, foreign goods and foreign banks, besides those related to Indian Equity/ Debenture issued for NRIs will, however, be accepted as far as the external services of All India Radio are concerned."
14. For example, without limiting the scope, the use of the following sound effects will not be permitted: rapid gunfire or rifle shots, sirens, bombardments, screams, raucous laughter, and the like.
15. Advertising and Children: Advertisements suggesting that a child may fail in his or her duty or lack in loyalty to any person or organisation if he/she does not buy their products and services or encourage others to do so, shall not be accepted.
16. No advertisement shall be accepted that leads children to believe that if they do not own or use the product advertised they will be inferior in some way to other children or that they are liable to be condemned or ridiculed for not owning or using it.
17. No advertisement likely to bring advertising into contempt or disrepute shall be permitted. Advertising shall not take advantage of the superstition or ignorance of the general public.
18. No advertising of talismans, charms and character reading from photographs, or such other matter as well as those which trade on superstition of general public shall be permitted.
19. Advertising needs to be truthful and should avoid distorting facts that could mislead the public by means of implications by false statements, as to the character of the merchandise, i.e. its utility, materials, ingredients, origin, etc.; the price of the merchandise, its value, its suitability or terms of purchase; the services accompanying purchase, including delivery, exchange, return, repair,

upkeep, etc.; personal recommendations of the article or service; the quality or the value of competing goods or trustworthiness of statements made by others.

20. Testimonials of any kind from experts, etc., other than government-recognized standardization agencies should not be permitted.
21. No advertisement shall be permitted to contain any claim so exaggerated as to lead inevitably to disappointment in the minds of the public.
22. Methods of advertising designated to create confusion in the mind of the consumer as between goods by one maker and another maker are unfair and shall not be used. Such methods may consist in; the imitation of the trademark of the name of competition or packaging or labeling of goods or the imitation of advertising devices, copy, layout, or slogans.
23. Indecent, vulgar, suggestive, repulsive or offensive themes or treatment shall be avoided in all advertisements. This also applies to advertisements which themselves are not objectionable as defined above, but which advertise objectionable books, photographs, or other matter and thereby lead to their sale and circulation.

Ensuring Transparency

Community radio is a reliable tool to monitor the access of rights and entitlements by the citizens in the broadcast area. The government and its various ministries, realizing the power of community radio to take the information to the last mile, have used the medium to promote its development programs and campaigns through community radio. In order to make the whole process transparent and more efficient, the government came up with the Central Plan Schemes Monitoring System on which civil society organizations registered themselves after making certain disclosures.

The Public Financial Management System (PFMS), earlier known as Central Plan Schemes Monitoring System (CPSMS), is a web-based online software application developed and implemented by the Office of Controller General of Accounts (CGA). PFMS initially started during 2009 as a Central Sector Scheme of Planning Commission with the objective of tracking funds released under all Plan schemes of GoI (Government of India), and real-time reporting of expenditure at all levels of program implementation. Subsequently in the year 2013, the scope was enlarged to cover direct payment to beneficiaries under both plan and non-plan schemes. An enhancement in the functionalities of PFMS commenced in late 2014, when it was envisaged that PFMS would digitalize accounts, and additional functionalities would be built into PFMS in stages.

The primary objective of PFMS is to facilitate a sound Public Financial Management System for Government of India by establishing an efficient fund flow system as well as a payment cum accounting network. PFMS provides various stakeholders with a real-time, reliable, and meaningful management information system and an effective decision support system as part of the Digital India initiative of GoI.

The biggest strength of PFMS is its integration with the Core Banking System (CBS) in the country. As a result, PFMS has the unique capability to push online payments to almost every beneficiary/vendor. At present, PFMS is able to interface with all public sector banks, regional rural banks, major private sector banks, Reserve Bank of India, India Post, and cooperative banks.

Nongovernmental organizations, being supported by funds from the central government ministries and departments, are also eligible for receiving payments through PFMS. Once a project comes to an end, the utilization documents and related information has to be uploaded online on the PFMS portal for further processing.

Per the directives from NITI Aayog, any new NGO can become eligible to receive funds through PFMS once it acquires an NGO Darpan ID post registering in the NGO Darpan website (http://ngo-darpan.gov.in/).

A case in point is the Department of Science and Technology, which supports CR stations with projects where they have to register themselves on the NGO Darpan portal. There are two modes by which any agency can be registered on PFMS:

1. Without logging in (applicable for receiving funds from central government only)
2. By logging in using credentials (for receiving funds from all other sources)

Community Radio Support Scheme

Sustainability has remained a cause of worry for community radio stations across the country. To promote sustainability and fund the stations for buying equipment and for capacity building, the government came up with the Community Radio Support Scheme with the aim to support stations in their work and operations. Community radio stations and letter of intent (LOI) holders may apply for financial assistance under the scheme "Supporting Community Radio Movement in India" facilitated by the Ministry of Information & Broadcasting.

Under the 12th Five Year Plan, Government of India has approved the scheme that seeks to provide financial assistance to **LOI** holders as well as operating community radio stations under the component, "Community Radio Support Scheme" (CRSS) for equipment acquisition, upgrades, and emergency grants.

The scheme strengthens new and existing community radio stations with resources, capacity, and technology thereby providing access and voice to marginalized communities; promote growth of CRS, especially in remote and rural areas, so that people living in these areas can have access to a meaningful medium of broadcast; and to promote the socioeconomic and cultural development of communities.

Grants under CRSS broadly cover the following areas:

(a) Equipment acquisition: capital expenditure for purchase and/or upgrade of equipment.

(b) Training support: to access training processes and facilities, build community capacity to produce content, and manage the CR process on their own.
(c) Emergency grants: to cover damages and repairs faced by community radio stations in extreme emergency situations like natural calamities, lightning, cyclone, etc.
(d) Replacement of existing equipment/upgrades/expansion as a one-time cost for existing (on-air) stations.
(e) Innovative grants: to support the community radio sector and encourage innovation in CR technology, content development, research, evaluation methodology development, and training processes, etc.

Further details can be obtained from the Ministry of Information and Broadcasting, Government of India website.

Another promising scheme supporting the setting up of community radios administered by the state governments is the Agricultural Technology Management Agency (ATMA) scheme that was launched during 2005–06, aiming at making the extension system farmer driven and farmer accountable by way of new institutional arrangements for technology dissemination in the form of an Agricultural Technology Management Agency (ATMA) at the district level to operationalize extension reforms. ATMA has active participation of farmers/farmer-groups, NGOs, Krishi Vigyan Kendras (KVKs), panchayati raj institutions, and other stakeholders operating at district level and below. Release of funds under the ATMA scheme is based on State Extension Work Plans (SEWPs) prepared by the state governments.

At present, the scheme is under implementation in 614 districts in twenty-eight states and three UTs in the country. In order to promote key reforms under the scheme, ATMA Cafeteria, 2010, continues to support activities in line with various policy parameters, including the support given to new community radio stations being set up by KVKs/SAUs or NGOs. Earlier, only KVKs and SAUs were included, but later NGOs were included under the scheme. ATMA schemes promote community radio by supporting the setup cost and three years of the programming cost of agricultural programs. Only one station in a particular district can be supported under ATMA.

Key Terms

Governance. The decision-making structures and processes associated with the implementation of a community radio station, all of which are expected to be transparent and participatory in nature.

Apex committee. Constituted by the licensing organization, this body takes care of licensing, annual maintenance of equipment, staff structure, budget, auditing, legal issues, and submission of necessary documents to government.

Content management committee. Consists mainly of people in and around the listening zone who take responsibility for broadcast content.

Ethics committee. Ensures maximum participation of the community and should see that the vested interests do not take control of the contents by offering financial support or by the use of political or muscle power.

Advisory body. Consists of members representing different sections of the concerned community, whose roles pertain to the operations of a community radio station, providing directions to ensure that community radio programming is relevant and interesting.

Management committee. The decision-making body for the community radio station that handles the radio setup and administrative and functional matters such as budgets, day-to-day programming, formulation of policies, technology, and human resources.

Vision and mission. Statements defining purpose and objectives serve as a foundational guide in the establishment of a community radio station.

Ministry of Information and Broadcasting. The Ministry that issues licenses and gives permission to set up a community radio station.

Indian Telegraph Act. States that the central government has the exclusive privilege of establishing and maintaining working telegraphs within India. The Act, and its subsequent amendments, define telegraph broadly to include most modern communication devices irrespective of their underlying technology.

WPC. Is The Wireless Planning & Coordination Authority wing of the Department of Telecommunications (DoT).

GOPA. Grant of permission agreement

WOL. Wireless operating license

3

Research and Analysis for Community Radio

Introduction: Media Research

This chapter moves from the governance processes to the research and analysis needed in community radio. Knowing the community and their needs are primary questions each community radio team must answer. This chapter throws light on how to conduct research on community needs and how to do pre and post project assessments to highlight changes in community attitudes and knowledge levels as well as sharing the various media research tools and methods employed.

Media research studies the development of media and related achievements and effects that include the methods used in collecting and analyzing information with regard to the content of newspapers, magazines, radio, television, cinema, and other mass media. The study of any medium of communication involves questions about the nature of the medium, how it works, what technology is involved, differences and similarities of the medium with other media, the services it provides, the costs, and whether the medium is effective and accessible, etc.

Media research involves collecting information about the uses and users of mass media. It is appropriate to ask how people use a medium or various media, whether it is for information and/or entertainment, education, etc.; what types of people use the different media more and why; what gratification the media provides; and what types of uses the media are put to.

Regarding radio, media research includes its uses, effects, and improvements in broadcasting technologies.

A Baseline Survey for Community Radio

Before establishing and signing the GOPA, the community radio license holder are advised to conduct a baseline survey (even though it is not mandatory) with at least 500 respondents from the broadcast zone. The objective is for the license holder to know the community and determine the available media options, their access to radio sets or phones with radio, program needs, media gap areas, availability of local expertise and talent, and the community's interest in participation in program production and broadcast. Baseline studies must be able to project and understanding of the local markets and its potential for revenue generation.

It is strongly advised that before launching the Community Radio station, the organisation to conduct a baseline community survey (model questionnaire is given in the annexure at the end of the book) and study the demography, its people, their media needs, media gaps, empowerment index etc.

A research report must be prepared and shared before signing the GOPA. A sample baseline report, as prepared by community radio *Alfaz-e-Mewat*, CR 107.8, is added.

It is most desirable to do this kind of study even before applying for a license and include a map of the local resources, businesses, industries, and special schemes so as to capitalize on them. The survey can help identify existing media gaps in terms of access and relevant content in the region, so these issues can be addressed in the process.

Major Aspects of Research

Research involves carefully designed procedures and a systematic process of study. All research studies have the following characteristics:

- Research is objective and verifiable. The data collected can be tested and validated.

- Research involves an empirical process. It is based upon empirical evidence or observable experiences. **It focuses on such problems that can be verified through empirical observation.**

In conducting research for a community radio station, identify the overarching objectives for which the community radio station would be set up.

Good research must be purposive. It must be carefully planned and timely executed. The researcher must have foresight. The research process requires an open mind and clarity of purpose. Everything must be planned with utmost precision. Objectives, hypotheses, and methodologies must be made clear beforehand.

Objectivity is the chief trait of all good research. **Personal biases must be kept from research studies.** The emphasis has to be on testing and finding out the ultimate reality.

We can accept something as truth when it is verifiable. Only then, it becomes credible.

Research is a professional effort involving systematic, accurate, and expert handling of the research problem. Data is gathered through systematic planning with control of data-collecting procedures. Data must be subjected to rigorous analysis. Any inferences or generalizations have to be stated in clear precise language.

A good research study focuses on facts. A balance must be struck between quantitative and qualitative facts. Facts are significant only when interpreted in the light of accepted standards and assumptions that are normative in character. Only by interpretation and evaluation methods that are determined by the purpose can facts relate to each other in a wider context.

Good research should contribute to widening knowledge and finding solutions to problems confronting society. Ethical questions are relevant and highly important in scientific research that is concerned with the discovery of truth.

Research for Monitoring

There are many reasons to undertake any study to determine the functioning of the community radio station and the level of acceptance it has received from the community. Some of the main reasons to conduct research for monitoring:

- Research helps to think rigorously and critically. Community radio operators become accustomed to carefully examining research evidence that is advanced for acceptance by the community and its listeners in a variety of popular and scholarly applications.
- The research process equips the research in learning how to find answers to questions facing the listeners group.
- Research contributes innovative ideas necessary for professional competence and growth.
- The researcher is able to understand radio listeners' program preferences and benefits associated with the program schedule.
- Researchers draw lessons from radio programs that work and those that do not work.
- Researchers can recommend strategies to further upscale the outreach of the CR.

Media Research Methods

People have always made enormous efforts to learn about the past, be aware of the present, and to probe into the future. Many have tried to understand, evaluate, and communicate their knowledge. This is the essence of research, particularly media research. Research is a systematic effort to secure answers to certain questions. In communications or media research, the questions are related to media that involves description, analysis, and interpretation of events and message-related behaviors.. Media research is done in a systematic manner typically adopting a specific methodology. The following methods are used in media research.

- Census
- Survey
- Observation
- Case study
- Interview
- Online real-time location-based research using a variety of web services
- Social media research

Quantitative Methods. Quantitative research concentrates on numbers. Such studies attempt to use precise statistical tools and models to achieve comprehensive understandings of communication behaviors and phenomena. The best examples of these are surveys and opinion polls. Such methods often try to predict present or future behavior in various communication situations. Quantitative methods help to provide precise explanations about processes and help measure communication behaviors.

Qualitative Methods. These methods depend on description and interpretation of meanings of communication messages by way of subjective treatment. Qualitative research concentrates on individual examples. Qualitative research does not try to find patterns. It makes intensive inquiries about single events, individuals, and social or communication units. Case studies and focus group studies are some examples of qualitative methods.

Census Method. This research method involves the study of the entire population or universe, covering every element of the universe. Thus the results are unbiased without prejudice. The census method is rarely used in media research because of the high cost, involvement of large manpower, with a lot of effort.

Survey Methods. In communication research, survey means looking at events, processes, and behaviors, etc., in their entirety. In communication research, a survey is an empirical study that uses questionnaires or interviews to discover descriptive characteristics of communication phenomena.

Surveys provides a limited amount of information from a large group of people and are useful when you want to learn what a larger population thinks. Though surveys can be used for all kinds of communication studies, there are two basic forms of surveys: questionnaire surveys and interview-based surveys.

Observation Methods. In media research, observation is perception with a purpose. The observation method usually looks into an occurrence, event, or phenomenon as it takes place. It is basically a qualitative method.

Participatory Observation. These non-experimental studies or inquiries are conducted as the subjects (people) are engaged in the natural course of their lives. Participatory observation is an important form of fieldwork. Researchers study groups by becoming a part of the group, trying to establish close relationships with the group members and observe and record their behavior. Such studies produce both qualitative and quantitative data.

Non-Participatory Observation. In participatory observation, researchers observe a group's behaviour from the outside and not as part of the group. Here the chances of getting personal details or behaviors are less. The interpretations are more or less objective. In participative observations, the researcher's sympathy and concerns are reflected in the interpretations.

Online Real-time Monitoring. This is possible only when the CR programs are also streamed on the internet or made available through a cell phone. Web-based software offers free and paid services to analyse the listener base, their listening habits, preferred listening times, amount of time spent on programs, etc. This method provides instant graphical representation of facts.

Sample Format of Baseline Survey Report (courtesy: S.M. Sehgal Foundation)

The report below gives a brief summary of the findings of the survey.

INTRODUCTION

Project Justification

Communication technologies have always been considered to be effective tools to bring about social inclusion and development. They vary from the simplest to the most complex means. The dawn of satellite transmission and wireless web technologies brought about a paradigm change for many, but there remains a large number of people who are voiceless as they do not have access to modern communication technologies. Hence the vital importance of area-specific communications in *choupals* (gathering places in a village) or folk forms of *nukkad natak* (performance art) and puppetry—these means still have a crucial role in development communications.

The traditional development approach has been a top-down focus on creating awareness in the community with the hope that critical information will trickle down, and community members will automatically absorb information important to them. However, it has been proven again and again in the grassroots that communities require a participatory approach, where they can make the decisions about what is necessary for their lives.

Community radio has played a revolutionary role in development communications worldwide since the late '70s, especially in Africa, Latin America, and North America. More recently, community radio has been heavily discussed in South Asia. In 2006, the Government of India gave the green light to establishing community radio stations in India for the first time.

Community radio is a low-cost technology model compared to others, which addresses access issues of the poorest communities. Further, it transcends literacy gaps and is known to encourage participation from all kinds of communities.

Description of a Target Group

The goal of an initiative by a non-government organization, S M Sehgal Foundation (Sehgal Foundation), to open up a new grassroots communication channel in the Mewat district in Haryana was to giving voice to the long-suppressed aspirations of the villagers and help transform rural India by bringing about a positive change in their lives.

Mewat district was carved out as a separate district in 2004 from the earlier parts of Gurgaon and Faridabad districts. Meo tribals are agricultural people with a distinct ethnic and socio-cultural history. The Meos, who trace their roots to the early Aryan invasion of Northern India, call themselves Kshatriyas and have preserved their social and cultural traits to a surprisingly large extent, unlike other tribes in nearby areas. During the reign of the Tughlaq dynasty in the fourteenth century AD, these formerly Hindu people embraced Islam. But they have maintained their age-old distinctive ethno-cultural identity.

Historically, the region has been extremely turbulent and subject to repeated invasions and resultant plundering throughout the post-Vedic period, largely due to the situational peculiarity of the area and the non-subjective attitude of the people. This led to a perceived "backwardness" and gross underdevelopment of the area and its people. The region has remained one of the "most underdeveloped regions" of India; even though it is located just about 70 kms from Delhi. The district forms part of the minority concentrated "most backward" ninety districts of India and scores extremely low in all socioeconomic indices of development.

The Original Development Objective

The Sehgal Foundation community radio project would address the problem of the widening communication gap between policy makers and villagers and the lack of access to mainstream media to give the community freedom of expression. The station would contribute to increasing the plurality and diversity of media in the area and enhance the capacities of communities to use media as a platform for furthering a participatory development process.

The community radio station will be run by the community, for the community, and be of the community. The overarching objectives with which the community radio will be set up are as follows:

1. Use radio as a tool for information dissemination especially in the area of policy, governance, and advocacy.
2. Use radio as an outreach tool for the grassroots.
3. Use radio as a tool for other educational purposes.
4. Preserve and promote the Mewati culture and language.

Immediate Objectives

A community radio station would engage local people in more than sixty villages in Nagina, Firozepur, Jhirka, and Punhana blocks of Mewat covering an approximate population of 220,000. The station would be operational by mid-2011.

Project Outputs

1. A trained cadre of volunteers from the community who manage and produce content for their community radio station.
2. A fully functional radio station that gives voice of the marginalised section of the society and brings them into the mainstream.
3. Bridge the gap between policy-makers and beneficiaries.

Activities

1. Capacity-building trainings on programming and technical skills
2. Studio design and acoustics
3. Purchase and installation of equipment
4. Promotional activities for CR station
5. Form listener groups

Project Inputs

1. Station equipment for a medium-sized community radio station.

2. Training and capacity building of volunteers on radio production, program planning, reporting, and editing of content.

INSTITUTIONAL FRAMEWORK ANALYSIS AND DISCUSSION

Gender and Age of Respondents

The majority of male respondents were interviewed in the survey. Almost 92 per cent respondents were male. Kherli, Madhi, Notki, Jalalpur, and Shadipur are villages where 10 per cent or more respondents were women, while in Kotla and Uletha all respondents were men.

Majority (almost 50 per cent) of the respondents are adult and middle-aged. Twenty per cent of the respondents were senior citizens (9 per cent) or below age twenty-one (11 per cent). Santhawadi, Lajalpur, Kherli, and Ghagas are the villages where the majority of respondents (more than 50 per cent) were adult and middle-aged.

Religion and Caste

The majority of the population in the survey villages are Muslim. Graph 3 shows that overall, 89 per cent of respondents are Muslim and the rest are Hindu. In Uletha and Jalalpur village, more than 20 per cent of respondents reported that they are Hindu. Only 3 per cent of households belong to a general caste category. The majority (87 per cent) of households belong to another "backward" caste category, while 10 per cent of households belong to a schedule caste category.

Education

More than one fourth of the respondents are illiterate while 15 per cent can read/write only. Apart from these respondents, 35 per cent of the population has primary or middle-level educational attainment. Only 20 per cent of the population has educational attainment up to matriculation (8 per cent), intermediate (6 per cent), and graduation or more

(6 per cent). Analysis reveals a lack of higher level studies in the population.

Occupation

The occupational status of the respondents showing in Graph 5 clearly indicates that the farming category is the major occupation and constitutes about 49 per cent of the total interviewed population. Twenty-three per cent of the respondents are laborers, 14 per cent are homemakers or students or are unemployed, 7 per cent are self-employed or established in a government or private job. The rest of the interviewed population are retired or have other occupations. Analysis reveals that agriculture is the main source of income in this region, and there are fewer opportunities available in the service sector.

Household Assets

Bar graph 9 indicates the domestic/movable assets owned by the interviewed households. About 70 per cent of the community residents have a mobile phone in their home, 42 per cent of the households has a two-wheeler, 35.2 per cent of the residents own bicycles, 35.8 per cent of the residents own coolers, 30.8 per cent of the residents own refrigerators, 12.4 per cent of the residents own radios, 9.2 per cent of households own tractors, and 7 per cent of households own televisions. A small proportion of households own washing machines, landline phones, CD players, a computer, and a four-wheeler.

Though a small proportion of households own televisions, a larger proportion of households own mobile phones. Overall, in 55–85 per cent of households, the respondent or a household member owns a mobile phone. The availability of mobile phones can be taken advantage of to spread information about community radio and programs through mobile messages and calls.

Almost two thirds of households own mobile phones and approximately one fourth of them have radio facility on their phones. Ten per cent of respondents reported that they have internet also on their mobile phones.

Government Scheme Implementation-Related Issues

The majority of households (80 per cent or more) raised their voices, saying that their area is neglected by local administration and they are unaware of various government schemes/programs. The population can be given more information about the available schemes and how to access them.

Access to Print Media

Access of print media is very little in this locality. A very small proportion of households have access to a newspaper or magazine. Approximately 7 per cent (one out of fifteen households) brought a newspaper, while one in 111 households brought a magazine into their home.

Access to Electronic Media

Television

Television can be accessed more readily than print media by an illiterate population. Overall, one in fifteen households in the survey area has a television. Among households with television, almost four fifths of the television sets are color and the rest are black-and-white. Among households with television, half have a cable connection, which means they have access to various television channels and the opportunity to gather/access more information.

Overall, more than one fifth of respondents stated that they watch television. Uletha is a village where more than 56 per cent of respondents watch television. In Ghagas, Santhawadi, Jalalpur, Notki, and Shadipur, one fourth of the respondents watch television. In Karheda and Madhi villages, very few respondents access television. In Kherli and Kotla villages, watching television by respondents is minimal.

News Channel

Consolidating the top three news channels accessed by respondents indicates that *Aaj Tak* and *Doordarshan (DD) News* are the only major channels viewed in the area. *Total News, Zee*

News, India TV, Today News, Aapki Duniya, Star News, Sahara Samay, Haryana News, IBN7, NDTV, 24-Hour News, etc., are also viewed by respondents but their numbers are far less.

In Jalalpur and Shadipur, *Total News* is also watched by the majority of respondents while in Ghagas, Kherli, and Madhi, *Zee News* is seen by many respondents.

Entertainment Channel

Overall, *Zee Cinema, Set Max* and *Star Utsav* and *Star Gold*, etc., are the major channels watched by respondents under the entertainment category. Some respondents also watch *Zee Action*, while others reported watching *Discovery, Zee TV, Zee Star, Star Plus, Star Utsav, Star Sports, Sab TV, Animal Planet, Ten Sports, Filmy, Sahara One, Urdu, Zee Classic, DD National* and *National Geographic*, etc., but the proportion of respondents watching these channels was minimal.

Except *Zee Cinema, Set Max, Star Utsav,* and *Star Gold*, all other channels viewed by respondents across all the villages have different levels of access.

Radio

Radio is the most popular means of entertainment. People can listen at work, while traveling, at home, etc. Availability of television sets, radio sets, and mobile radios in the village reveals that radio is more popular than television. Data shows that ten in every eighty-one households own a radio set. The entire surveyed village except Kotla had an adequate number of radio sets. Earlier analysis revealed that ten in every forty-one respondents who own mobile phones reported having radio facility available in their mobile handset.

More than one fifth of respondents reported that they access radio anywhere and anytime. Ghaghas, Kotla, and Uletha are the villages where more than one fourth of respondents access radio, while in Karheda, Jalalpur, Notki, and Santhawadi, about one fifth of respondents listen to radio. Shadipur village has the fewest radio listener respondents.

More than half of the respondents who access radio are frequent listeners of radio programs. Forty per cent of respondents are daily listeners, while one third of respondents access radio less frequently.

Ghaghas and Kotla are the villages where the proportion of less-frequent radio listening respondents is high, while in Uletha the majority of respondents access radio less frequently. Among the rest of the villages, the majority of respondents are frequent radio listeners.

The majority of respondents prefer night time (8:00 p.m.–10:00 p.m.) for radio listening In the morning (6:00 a.m.–10:00 a.m.) about one fifth of respondents listen to radio.

In all the villages except Kherli and Madhi, most of the respondents prefer nighttime for radio listening, but in Jalalpur, Karheda, Kherli, Kotla, Madhi, Santhawadi, and Uletha, more than one fourth of radio listener respondents prefer morning (6:00 a.m.–10:00 a.m.) for radio listening.

Preferred timings for listening to radio suggest allocating broadcast timings. Morning (after 6:00 a.m. to before 10:00 a.m.) and evening (after 6:00 p.m. to before 10:00 p.m.) would be ideal for broadcasting the community channel in the area.

FM and MW/SW are the main bands that have been accessed by the respondents. All the villages except Shadipur and Uletha have some respondents who listen to community radio, though the number listening to other channels is higher than community radio. But it should be related to FM or MW/SW, and it has been reported as a sports channel.

Home is the main place for listening to radio. With neighbors at a *choupal* (gathering place in village) is the second major place for listening to the radio according to respondents. In Santhawadi, Jalalpur, and Kherli villages, at least twelve of 100 respondents listen radio at their workplace.

The majority of respondents listen to radio for news updates (85 per cent) and sports news (65 per cent). Except for Kherli, Kotla, and Uletha, a small proportion of respondents from all the villages listen to interactive sessions/phone-in programs. Other favorites reported by respondents are *RJ/Anchor*, local community updates, updates on traffic and market rates, new things, etc., but the number of respondents accessing these favorites is far less.

Almost 40 per cent of the respondents stated that a radio channel asks for feedback. Fifteen per cent of respondents said that radio programs have an impact on their lives with regard to education, job-related information, agriculture, and health-related information.

Participation in Media Programs

None of the respondents had ever participated in any radio or television programs. A very small number of respondents had participated in theater and/or singing competitions, and these respondents are from Ghagas, Karheda, and Notki villages.

More than half of the respondents were willing to participate in proposed community radio programs. Education, agriculture, and rural development were the most frequently reported subject/issues where respondents were willing to participate in the future. Health, music, and theatre are issues that one to two fourths of respondents showed their willingness to participate. Almost 10 per cent of respondents stated other preferences for participation in sports, employment, and spiritual programs.

Conclusions/Observations

- Two thirds of surveyed households practice open defecation, and they do not have access to a toilet facility. Construction of a toilet and its use will be a good hygiene and sanitation issue for radio programs.
- Smoke from solid cooking fuels is a serious health hazard. A high percentage of households use firewood (98.2 per cent) and dung cakes (81.8 per cent) as cooking fuel. The proportion of households using LPG (2.8 per cent) and kerosene (9.1 per cent) are much fewer. Information on the usage of safe fuel can be given on the radio.

- The population in the study area has fewer interactions or associations outside the household with any group or local panchayat. Formation of self-help groups (SHG) and their benefits, and as well as creating an awareness about Panchayati Raj, its roles and responsibilities, can be spread through community radio.
- A majority of households (80 per cent or more) raised their voices, saying that their areas are neglected by local administration, and they are unaware of various government schemes/programs. The population can be given more information about the available schemes and ways to access their benefits.
- Radio (21.4 per cent) is more popular than television (7 per cent), newspapers (7 per cent), and magazines (1 per cent) in the study area. At the same time, 21 per cent of respondents stated that their mobile phones have a radio facility. More than half of the respondents listen to radio frequently.
- Preferred listening times for radio suggest allocating/broadcasting timings. Mornings (after 6:00 a.m. to before 10:00 a.m.) and evenings (after 6:00 p.m. to before 10:00 p.m.) would be ideal for broadcasting in the area.
- Home is the main place for listening to radio. The *choupal* (a gathering place in the village) is the second major place for listening to radio as reported by respondents.
- More than half of the respondents were willing to participate in proposed community radio programs. Education, agriculture, and rural development are the most frequently reported subjects/issues respondents are willing to participate with in the future. Health, music, and theatre are the issues that up to half of respondents showed their willingness to participate in. Almost 10 per cent of respondents stated other preferences for participation, which included sports, employment, and spiritual programs.

- Those who are willing to participate in the future community radio programs can be positioned as volunteer-based as their preference for participation. These volunteers can spread information about timings and topics of the radio programs within the community.
- More than one fifth of respondents are associated with Sehgal Foundation across all the enumerated villages, while in Kherli, Madhi, and Shadipur villages, none of the respondents are associated with Sehgal Foundation. As the respondents from most of the villages are aware of Sehgal Foundation, that will help Sehgal Foundation spread awareness among communities about the launch of a community radio station.

Key Terms

Research. The term suggests an attitude of enquiry—an honest, intelligent, and exhaustive quest for facts—the unknown and the known. It is a systematic way of collecting, classifying, and analyzing either quantitative or qualitative information.

Baseline Survey. A "reality check" for the license holder to know the community, the available media options, access to radio, program needs, media gap areas, availability of local expertise and talent, their interest in participation in the program production and broadcast, and more.

Benefits of Research. Research contributes to new facts and generalizations. It keeps the professional researcher abreast with the latest in their discipline. Research creates an urge for taking further strides in one's discipline. It modifies partial theories and helps dispel myths and antiquated practices by examining them on the anvil of scientific validity.

4

How to Set Up a Community Radio Station

Introduction

Community Radio Stations (CRS) in India have played a major role in educating and encouraging the remote societies. India has 235+ CRS in rural and urban areas benefiting the societies, and there is a need for more stations.

Chapter Structure
❍ Steps to Start a Community Radio
❍ Structure of a Community Radio
❍ Cost of a Studio
❍ Convergence
❍ Digitalization

Steps to Start a Community Radio

- Who can apply? Licenses can be given only to three categories, i.e. educational institution (college/university), NGO and Krishi Vigyan Kendra (KVK). These bodies should be functional for at least five years. So, if you want to start up a CRS as a private institution or organisation, you need a recommendation from the district administration (as per amendment August 2018). Further, the private institutions or organisations wanting to set up a CR station in LWE-affected areas/border areas will also provide site security clearance for installation at the proposed geo coordinates from local administration. For educational institutes and government universities and KVKs, there is a single clearance window.

- NGOs/registered societies and public charitable trusts shall be registered on Niti Aayog's darpan portal, and the applicant shall provide its unique ID along with application.

Know your community and vision for setting up a CRS: The reason will also include details of the target audience and target area. With all these details in place, the proposal can be sent to the Ministry of Information and Broadcasting.

- First make an application either offline or online by downloading the application form available from the website of Ministry of Information and Broadcasting. As of March 2019, seven copies of the applications along with a fee in the form of Demand Draft (might change into online soon) for Rs. 2500/- on the name of the person specified in the application guidelines. The applicant must be sure of the location in which he wants to set up the transmitter tower and its geo coordinates. In case of private and Civil society organisations, the applicant must be routed through District administration . The location of the tower also to be approved by the District administration.
- The ministry does the preliminary screening and sends it to various other counter parts like Home, Defense, HRD, Agriculture, WPC wing of the Department of Telecommunications etc.
- Once the ministry gets the nod from these agencies it might either be referred to the screening committee notified by the ministry to call for personal interactions (valid for private and civil society organisations) and to the Inter ministerial committee (in the case of Govt. owned educational institutions and Krishi Vigyan Kendras).

- Once cleared by these committees, the applicant is issued a letter of intent (LOI) by the Ministry of Information and Broadcasting.
- On receipt of the LOI, the applicant applies for a Frequency allocation to the WPC wing of the Department of Telecommunication. This should be done within 30 days.
- WPC then issues another Letter of Intent to the applicant asking them to pay a prescribed spectrum charges (Rs. 22500/- per year). This should be done online and the hard copy to be sent to them.
- The applicant then applies for SACFA (Standing Advisory committee for Frequency Allocation) to the WPC. This simply means getting a NOC from major spectrum users in the region.
- Once the SACFA clearance is received, the applicant signs a GOPA agreement with the Ministry of Information and Broadcasting
- Applicant then finalises the vendor through which he proposes to buy the transmitter.
- After setting up the studio and transmitters, the applicant applies for the Wireless operating License called WOL along with the Invoice, and a copy of GOPA.
- Once the WOL is received, one can start the transmission of radio programmes. But it should be ensured that the station should be on AIR within 90 days of signing of GOPA.

Structure of a Community Radio

A radio station involves many technology components. Inside a studio, minimum requirements include a mixer, a mic, a computer, and a pair of headphones. A computer is used for audio transmission when the station is live and for audio editing. Stations usually use more than one computer for different tasks. As the radio station grows , more components can be added for telephony for people to call the radio station and for internet connectivity to stream the content on the net. A startup CRS requires only a minimum space of ten-by-ten-foot room. Two to three desktops, a console for operating radio, and an editing room fulfil the basic infrastructure requirements in a studio, plus a station manager and one to two RJs (radio jockeys) or volunteers for jockeying. There are several options available for playout systems, including Gram Vaani's GRINS box that helps in scheduling, archiving, and telephony at the station.

Studio Configuration as Described by BECIL

On-Air Studio. The basic requirement of a community radio station is for a common "on-air" and "program production studio," which will be acoustically treated. The equipment complement will meet the requirements of recording, editing, and storage in the analog and digital domains, besides meeting the requirements of an "on-air studio." The recording and playback facilities will center around a hard-disk-based system assisted by compact disc and cassette players, etc.

Voice-Over Booth (Discussion Studio). The next step is to include a voice-over booth (VOB) in addition to the On-Air Cum Production Studio. VOB is an acoustically treated booth designed to optimize the requirements of spoken word programming. The room will be suitable to accommodate four participants, and the proceedings from there can either be recorded or put live on the air through the on-air studio. Provision is available for participants to listen to the programs on high-quality headphones.

Production Studio. A separate production studio can be provided for stations where more quantum of in-house production is anticipated. The production studio will be equipped with recording/editing and storage devices. This will enable uninterrupted production activities even while the station is on the air. The production studio can also serve the purpose of a backup studio for on-air studio in case of emergency.

Transmitter Configuration

The most important and tedious job while setting up a CRS is getting a transmitter, referred to as "the soul" of CRS. The government has to be informed and provide permission before obtaining a transmitter. It is important to note that even If the transmitter is sold or scrapped later, the government needs to be notified. Two types of transmitters are used: local and imported. As a good practice, most CRSs have a backup transmitter in case the first transmitter stops functioning.

Major components in a transmitting chain consist of a transmitter, an antenna, a feeder cable, and a tower. Various combinations can, therefore, be worked out to suit individual requirements, keeping in view the availability of funds. These combinations will, however, revolve around the following parameters.

- Maximum Effective Radiated Power: 100 W
- Configuration: Single or 1 + 1, minimum permitted height of antenna above ground is fifteen meters; maximum permitted height of antenna above ground is thirty meters.

Another important step is building a tower for the transmitter. This requires experts for setting up the transmitter.

Following is a quick snapshot of tasks performed or associated with each of the technological components at the radio station.

Cost of a Studio

Costs involved in launching a community radio station depend upon facilities to be provided and may range between 9 lakhs to 30 lakhs and more. Three modules are described in the following paragraphs for the purpose of illustration.. A combination of various transmission and studio facilities can be used depending on the requirements.

Basic Studio. The basic setup consists of a minimum complement of equipments required to set up a radio station.

This module can be designed on the concept of a common on-air and program production studio to be acoustically treated to provide an optimum reverberation time. The recording and playback facility will center around a CD player and cassette recorder/MD recorder. Automated playout system through a computer can be added for a nominal extra cost. The transmission facility can be designed around a single 50 watt professional-grade transmitter with a single element roof-mounted antenna.

Mid-Range Studio. The mid-range studio setup can be designed to include a voice-over booth (VOB) in addition to the one studio of basic setup. VOB is an acoustically treated booth designed to optimize the requirements of spoken-word programming. The room has to be suitable to accommodate four participants, and the proceedings from there can either be recorded or put live on air through the on air studio. The transmission facility can be designed around a single 50 watt professional-grade transmitter with a two-element antenna mounted on a 30-meter-high self-supporting tower.

High-End Studio. The high end setup can be designed for stations where more quantum of in-house production is anticipated. For this purpose an additional production studio with necessary equipments has to be provided to meet the requirement The high-end module will enable uninterrupted production activities even while the station is on the air. The production studio can also serve the purpose of a backup studio or "on-air studio" in case of emergency. The transmission facility can be designed in a 1+1 configuration of 50 watt professional-grade transmitters.

Convergence

Convergence (internet and/or telephony) can be both beneficial and dangerous to community radio stations depending on usage and context. On the one hand, once the initial cost of the production is paid for, the actual digital replication can go on with minimal expense. On the other hand, the content travels from an autonomous and independent infrastructure to privately owned infrastructures, thereby becoming vulnerable to intellectual property rights and/or copyright regimes. The cultural and economic aspects of this convergence are sensitive issues for community radio stations. Of course, the FM radio listenership itself doesn't invoke costs.

However, the linear nature of analog broadcasting means that there will always be a substantial number of listeners who will miss the program. Telephony can be a convenient and interactive way of staying in touch with the local community radio stations. Integration with telephony can more than triple a community radio's interaction with listeners. However, telecommunication infrastructure is involved, and the listener or the station usually incurs the cost. If the radio incurs the cost, participation remains high. If the user incurs the cost, then participation will dip to some extent. Telephony, including social media, makes the radio programs interactive; it is the listener's voice that enters the studio. Once the listener's voice is available in digital format, it attains different kinds of values for different stakeholders—experts, advertisers the radio station, aid agencies, researchers, etc. Radio stations need to build capacities for how to engage with quantified participation in terms of ethics and intellectual property rights as well as build further awareness around these issues for their listeners. CR stations might sign agreements with telecom and/or internet service providers for zero rating, reduced call rates, or toll-free calls, etc. With the availability of data through all devices including low-cost feature phones, community radio should also look into convergence. With most operators as of September 2018 offering 1GB per day as the minimum data, it is worthwhile to stream the signals through the internet. A common mobile app will also help to enlarge the listenership.

Digitalisation

The digitalisation of cable and of terrestrial medium-wave public service, broadcasting has already achieved significant technical progress, although it is not clear what financial or social benefits have been achieved.

There are two major modes of digital radio that are used by users: Digital Radio Mondiale (DRM) and Digital Audio Broadcasting (DAB All India Radio uses DRM to phase out the AM and SW transmitters. But the government is yet to make a decision on digital frequencies for the commercial and community sectors. Digital radio will make frequencies easier to allot. The same transmitter can be used for multiple radio stations. The power of the transmission could be altered depending on the need and time of broadcasts. Within the next decade, India hopes to phase out analog transmission and embrace 100 per cent digitalisation. Many nations have already embraced digitisation.

Transition to digital broadcasting will undoubtedly require existing broadcasters and future applicants to mobilise a much greater capital investment, especially the transmission equipment. Until digital radio transmitters are not as affordable as analog FM transmitters, radio stations should have their transmission equipment completely subsidised or shared through the Community Radio Support Scheme. For a smooth transition to digital radio, there is a need to ensure a period of simulcasting.

Visual Radio

The fruits of digital technology lie in its innovative adaptation by the users. Most TV programs and audio uploads use platforms like YouTube, which consumes bandwidth of a video program. The program uses a bandwidth of 1 GB for an audio feed of 13 Mbps. Spoken-word TV programs like interviews and discussions are audio programs showing the faces of the participants along with some texts and graphics. Digital radio is enough to convey the same effect. It is economical for the producer as well as the user. Hence community radio stations, while producing community radio programs, will also work toward "visual radio" as they attempt to stream it online. One of the authors of this book introduced the concept of radio vision using world space technology in 2002. Some programs were produced and aired as part of a UNESCO India publication.

Key Terms

GOPA. Grant of Permission Agreement (GOPA), which authorizes the license holder to operate a CRS for five years.

On-Air Studio. An acoustically treated room that hosts the recording and playback facilities that center around a hard-disk-based system assisted by compact disc and cassette players, etc.

Voice-Over Booth (Discussion Studio). An acoustically treated booth designed to optimize on the requirements of spoken-word programming.

Production Studio. Used by staff for program making, editing, and is equipped with recording/editing and storage devices.

DRM. Digital Radio Mondiale.

DAB. Digital Audio Broadcasting.

5

Formats of Radio Programs

Introduction

This chapter describes the methods to adopt when deciding a radio format and the various types of radio formats and programs. This will include new formats that have emerged from the easy access to telephony and other telecommunication facilities and with the integration of social media with conventional radio.

The previous chapters helped explain how a radio station works. Newspaper is heterogenous. There is the first page, color supplements, classified advertisements, editorials, special features, regional news, national news, international news, sports news, Bollywood happenings, and the famous "Page 3" that talks about social gatherings. A radio station also broadcasts programs of different varieties which includes spoken word, interviews, discussions, classical music, folk music, light music, drama, documentaries, quiz programs, etc. Such programs are called formats.

Chapter Structure

- Spoken Word or Human Voice
- Music
- Sound Effect
- Other Radio Formats
- Formats of the Future

Deciding a Format

When considering the coverage area of a radio station, a survey provides an insight into the target community. Demographic data are available. Their media gaps are visible. The station knows their vocabulary, language, and method by which a large number of people within the community understand a particular subject. The spoken dialect and local folk arts are important. When an issue is identified, preliminary discussions between the producer and the target audience with regard to the themes, contents, and message take place. Availability of experts in the region also determines the format. Most of what is spoken on radio is written down before it's spoken. This is generally referred to as "scripted." Each radio program has three ingredients.

1. Spoken Word or Human Voice
2. Music
3. Sound Effects

Spoken Word or Human Voice

Announcements. People who have listened to All India Radio may be familiar with standard announcements that include the time, the name of the radio station, the mode and the frequency, the name of the program, the name of the artist and the names of the production team and those making the announcements are the announcers.

Compering. If the announcers do some homework and start by giving an introduction to a program with details about the artists and perhaps some insights into the music used, etc. and also link programs that follow one another, then they are called comperes.

Anchoring. There is a slight difference between a compere and an anchor. The latter also takes into account the mood and type of the audience and is typically more informal.

Radio Jockey (RJ). This term of recent origin refers to a one-man/woman radio show where the host is expected to be with the listeners for a few hours. The RJ multitasks and is often expected to be a jack of all trades. RJs perform special shows based on personality that results in them becoming a celebrity of sorts.

Talk. Radio talk is probably the oldest format on radio. There has been a tradition in India and Britain to invite experts or prominent people to speak for ten to fifteen minutes on a specific topic. These talks go through a process of being changed into radio's spoken word style. India had hour-long discourses such as *Harikatha, Burrakatha*, etc. Correspondence course students from Delhi or Madurai or Patiala listened to half-hour lectures on the radio. The listening span of a single voice has reduced over time, so the talks became shorter and shorter. Talks became talklets and then snippets. This form is often used by public service broadcasters.

Interviews. Types of interviews differ in terms of their duration, content, and purpose. One-to-one, one-to-many, many-to-one, etc. Interviews can be conducted by the studio anchor or an interviewer. They can take the shape of question-and-answer programming. Interviews can be phone-in or phone out and may also be done in the field. The duration of these may vary from ten to thirty minutes or even sixty minutes depending on the topic and the person being interviewed. Most of such interviews are personality based. Interviews are used in various radio documentaries to obtain very brief, to-the-point answers.

Another type of interview-based program puts across one or two questions to ordinary people or those with knowledge on some current topic to measure public opinion. Such programs are called "vox pop" (Latin meaning "voice of people."). There are basic do's and don'ts when conducting any interview and sample do's include being courteous and respectful.

Discussions. Electronic media and TV news channels have made this format very popular. Through discussion, solutions to problems can be found. In any discussion, two or three or even a dozen people discuss a particular issue or event, and a moderator or anchor comes to a conclusion. Radio discussions are produced especially when there are controversial social or economic issues. When different experts meet and discuss such issues, people can understand various points of view. 139

Documentaries/Features. Documentaries can be divided into two types: one a well-researched, studio-based, voice-modulated program with background music and sound effects. This can be about a social cause, history, a tradition, health habits, diseases, etc. A second type are radio documentaries based on field-based recordings. They may be based on voices from the field, opinions expressed by experts, or both. Features can be produced based on places, festivals, or on natural calamities such as cyclones, floods, drought, tsunami, earthquake, or man-made disasters like terrorist attacks, they need to be factual and neutral.

Radio Reports. These are based on some events recorded earlier, edited, and broadcast by the stations,such as radio newsreels on current affairs.

Drama. A radio drama or a radio play is like any other play staged in a theater or entertainment venue. The only difference is that while a stage play has actors, stage, sets, curtains, properties movement, and live action, a radio play has only three components: the human voice, music, and sound effects. Radio drama uses the power of imagination and suggestion. Radio plays can trigger the imagination of the listener and no two listeners will have the same image.

Running Commentaries. Ardent fans of a sport such as cricket, who travel, would like to follow the match and radio can make this possible; even while doing routine work one can listen to radio commentary using a headphone. In addition to giving play by play commentary, this format is also used to provide eyewitness accounts of special events such as Independence Day and Republic Day celebrations, festivals, Kumbh Mela, as well as public homage to departed leaders or for covering Satellite launches.

Magazine programs. Radio magazines are replicas of weekly/fortnightly/monthly magazines like '*Time Newsweek*, *India Today*, *Outlook*, etc. Magazines presented by a celebrity or a popular anchor will have special interviews, discussions, storytelling, music, reports of special events, quiz programs, jingles, etc. The duration of a magazine program is thirty minutes with five to ten smaller segments that might encompass many radio formats. Some radio magazines like *Namaskar Bhopal* or breakfast shows of some stations may run for two hours.

News. News is the most popular format of radio. Unbiased facts and double-checked news with excellent voices and perfect diction was the order of erstwhile radio. Views were packed as current affairs programs. News reels and radio reports contained recordings from actual events. But hardcore news is not allowed in community radio. Soft news must be mainly educational, developmental, and/or cultural on community radio.

Music

Radio is synonymous with music. In the earlier decades, music in radio was mostly classical and traditional, but the growth and popularity of Bollywood and the Indian cinema has brought it to the center stage. Use of commercial music is governed by copyright and intellectual property laws. Even the use of commercial music for background effects is governed by the law. The user has to sign agreements with agencies that hold the music rights. Broadcasting of commercial music is becoming expensive and difficult. Community radio stations must attempt to create original music in all its forms.

Sound Effects

Sound effects play a major role in creating interest among listeners. Even silence plays an important role in radio programs. Sound effect banks are available free of cost as well as for a royalty fee. Original background music is mixed to provide the mood and ambience of a program.

New Radio Formats

India has taken giant leaps in the field of information technology, and radio as a medium has taken a lead in applying information technology in its broadcasts. Let us discuss some of these formats:

Phone in Program. In an age of technological development, phone-in is a most-important format. This interactive programming involves the listener and the presenter talking to each other. Their talk goes on air instantly. The listener has the satisfaction that his voice is being listened to and responded to immediately. Other listeners also pay attention. Such presentations require advance publicity so that listeners can prepare to air their grievances/queries or requests. They dial up the announced telephone number at a stipulated time and their problems are discussed with experts in the studio. Initially this format was introduced for playing listener requests based on popular songs. But it is being used for health-related programs, rural broadcasts, and for voicing complaints against the government/ administrative machinery, etc.

Radio Bridge/Teleconferencing. Radio bridge means connecting different stations throughout the length and breadth of the country. An expert sitting at Chennai can interact with the common man in a studio in Delhi. This format was first used by All India Radio during elections.

Voicemail. People are not always in a position to participate in phone-in programs due to the long wait times and/or non-availability of the links. So experts tend to receive some unwanted calls or calls of less significance. The use of voicemail-based radio programs gives the listener the opportunity to record his question at any time. The producer has a chance to go through the questions, views, etc., classify them and also edit them if needed.

Social Media. The advent of social media platforms such as Google audio, Facebook audio conferencing, Skype conferencing, and Whatsapp group calls provide an opportunity for radio producers to develop new formats in broadcasting with more participation and interaction without incurring additional costs.

Formats of the Future

Digital Media. With the availability and accessibility of data being made economical and easier, radio can easily become visual. Basic pictures, photos of the presenter and participants, graphs, and data can be projected on mobile screens as well as computing equipment. More innovative formats of audio with visual supplements are needed.

Innovative Formats. Radio can easily provide the largest screen on earth—the sky—through programs on Sky Watching. People can listen to the audio and watch the sky and understand nature.

Convergent Formats. Radio stations can join hands with developmental agencies and send printed pamphlets about programs and create a greater sense of curiosity among listeners. The program might later encourage the audience to practice some of the knowledge advocated in the program by providing access to institutions as well as providing interactive participatory kits.

Key Terms

Radio Formats. Refers to the overall content broadcasting of a radio station. Many radio formats are designed to reach a specifically defined segment or niche of the listening population based on demographic criteria such as age, ethnicity, background, etc.

Spoken word. Spoken words on radio are written down, or generally referred to as "scripted."

Music. Use of commercial music is governed by copyright and intellectual property laws. The user must sign agreements with agencies who hold the music rights and pay a fee when their music used. Community radio stations must attempt to create original music whenever possible.

Convergent media. The interconnection of information and communications technologies, computer networks, and media content.

Intellectual Property Rights. Intellectual property refers to creations of the mind: inventions; literary and artistic works; and symbols, names, and images used in commerce.

Copyright. Copyright is the right to copy. The original creator of a product (writing, music, image, etc.) and anyone given authorization to are the only ones with the exclusive right to reproduce the work.

6

Financial Sustainability

Introduction

The community radio model differs from nation to nation. The word "community" suggests non-commercial radio. The model has to differ from commercial radio and public radio. The latter of course is funded from taxpayer money, be it in the nature of government grants or licensing fees. But funding from international aid agencies and charitable institutions has steadily decreased in recent years. Each station has to develop its own marketing strategy and business model for the survival and sustenance of community radio.

As of October 1, 2018, there are 238 radio stations in India, and out of those, only a a few are performing extremely well .No doubt, certain community radio stations cross the line and tend to be more commercial. This is possible in zones where there are no clear FM signals of either the public broadcaster or commercial stations. This chapter deals with successful marketing strategies.

Advertisements (Government, etc.)

Advertisement in any medium presupposes the number of people to be reached through that medium. Eyeballs or normal hits determine the advertisement rates. But like television rating points (TRPs) and Broadcast Audience Research Council (BARC) ratings, community radio does not have a mechanism to understand its reach. In community radio it is not the numbers that make it useful, it is the changes it creates in the society. The latter is a long-term benefit, and there are not enough measurable tools.

Even though 2006 guidelines stated that community radio stations were allowed to broadcast commercials for up to five minutes per hour, the idea did not take off. Then it was left to a committee headed by Dr. Brahmananda Brahma, chief economic advisor, and members such as Dr. Sreedher. Sunit Tandon, after visiting some CR stations and understanding the efforts taken by them in marketing their stations, recommended to the government that the Directorate of Audio Visual Publicity (DAVP) could release social advertisements at a minimum rate of one rupee per second for community radio stations. The stations would first have to go through a empanelment procedure by sending their GOPA, WOL, and three months of programming.

A simple calculation: If a station broadcast eight hours a day, they were eligible for forty minutes commercial time or 2,400 seconds per day. One rupee per second amounts to 2,400 per day. For thirty days, it comes to 72,000 rupees. A station can easily run on its own provided it gets commercials for one rupee per second.

Later in 2009, another committee was formed under Dr. Brahma and Dr. Sreedher with functional radio stations presenting their budget estimates. The government decided to hike the rates to four rupees per second. As of 2018, ninety-nine community radio stations have been empaneled with DAVP. If they could market commercials at this rate, it works out to Rs. 280,000 per month—a good amount to run a station. In 2017, the government enhanced the duration of commercials to 7.5 minutes per hour.

State governments such as Kerala also empaneled community radio stations and released advertisements at rates that were normally more than the DAVP rates.

DAVP also prescribed production of local programs on national themes by allowing the stations to produce them on their own. A sum of Rs. 6,000 would be paid for a thirty-minute program for projects lasting up to ninety episodes. If the department funded more than ninety and up to 180 programs, the rates were 5,000 per half hour. For a year-long program, stations were provided with Rs. 4,000 per half hour. DAVP adopted the rates followed by the Department of Science and Technology through its flagship programs, Science for Women and Radio Mathematics.

Social Messages/Advertisements (Aid Agencies and Charitable Organizations)

There is no fixed rate for these messages. Many international organisations such as WHO, FAO, UNICEF, etc., are engaged in implementing the Millennium Development Goals adopted by the United Nations. Some money is available under IEC budgets for campaigns.

Advertisements (Local)

Immense possibilities exist for local advertisements. But the majority of stations are yet to tap these sources. A survey on the advertising potential of the business community in the listening zone must to be conducted. A radio station in Odisha collects only 100 rupees from a shopkeeper per month and the same amount from fifty other shop owners. The shops get mentioned during the radio programs at least twice a day. This model can be replicated by other stations.

If the station made a database of all the people in the listening zone, with their birthdays, marriage anniversaries, child births, and deaths, these days could be observed on the radio possibly charging just ten rupees per message.

The local temple festivals or events in the mosques and churches could be covered, and the radio can become a media partner. The radio station gets visibility, listeners, and a sponsorship fee.

Micro and Nano Commercials

Following the above mentioned ideas, even a five-second mention of a product or branding of time checks could generate income.

Subscription and Membership Fees

There are innumerable models for subscriptions. The Deccan Development Society and Sangam Radio are examples. Jamia Millia Islamia used to collect radio fees from students. Many listeners' clubs charge an annual membership fee.

Projects

The ministries and departments of the Government of India have short-term and long-term campaigns such as the Drive against Polio, Clean India, Save the Girl Child, Communal Harmony, National Integration, Voter Awareness, Consumer Rights, Health and Family Welfare, Nutrition, Women's health, Science Popularisation, etc. They release jingles and spots as advertisements. By organising workshops and seminars and providing guidelines and content, stations can produce the program. Even though the DAVP has a fixed rate, it is up to the donor agency to decide on the nature of funding.

Besides government projects, Corporate Social Responsibility (CSR) funding from corporates is available for projects benefiting the listener community. It is important to note that radio cannot become the mouthpiece or a tool of propaganda for a company or its product but only the social project it is supporting. Sponsorship of programs are allowed only by the government departments and public-sector undertakings.

Digital Services

With web streaming and mobile apps, community radio's coverage area covers the entire globe. But the purpose is defeated by enhancing the reach. With the availability of data and gadgets among the common people, it is not a bad idea to have community radio signals web streamed. Certain digital platforms (like Google, and Youtube) actually pay if the listeners exceeds a certain number. It is more effective to link the live streaming through social media (like Facebook and Twitter) to enhance visibility. The more listeners, the more likely an advertiser offers money. Proximity is an important factor. The Indian diaspora would like to listen to events closer to their home, village, district and state. It is possible for them to spare some money for running the radio station.

Hiring of Studios and Infrastructure

The studio infrastructure will be largely unutilised except during live broadcasts or compering. Out of twenty-four hours, barely 10 per cent of the facilities will be in use. Studios may be rented out for voice-over recording and dubbing for documentary filmmakers, amateur singers, folk singers, local marketers, etc. The office with telecom facilities may be used to host community service centers of the government, public sector enterprises, or social service organisations. If there are three listeners for community radio in a particular space (which is theoretically possible), all three can share the same tower to host their antennas and transmitter, and thereby reduce the cost of generators, UPS, security, etc.

Production and Marketing Audio Albums

The station might use the studios for creating individual music albums for folk artists and local musicians, and also provide a centralised platform for their sale.

Internships (Journalism and Mass Communication Students)

More than 1,000 journalism and mass communication departments are attached to various universities, colleges, and business establishments. But the stress is on public relations, advertising, investigative journalism, film production, acting, music production, documentaries, etc. But adequate no place offers training in development communication in community radio. These stations might consider allowing interns and also charge fees for internships or to produce programs at little or no cost. Some stations charge a fee for school/college students to visit the radio station.

Exchange Programs and Archives

Stations could create an audio archive and share their programs with other like-minded stations in the region. Common programs like music, health, etc., could be shared, thereby reducing the cost and increasing the visibility.

Competitions

Stations can organise quiz competitions or contests among school children or college students and institute prizes. Some nominal fee could be charged, or other institutions could be asked to host or co-host the program.

Research

Stations with trained volunteers can offer local surveys to be undertaken for government and non-government establishments, thereby providing a window for marketing agencies in the coverage area. The station could conduct radio surveys by inviting responses from callers directly on the studio number.

Community Radio Sustenance Fund

The fund offers support for creating of 100 hours of programming each year at the cost of Rs. 2,500 per hour for community radio stations. In addition to program funding, the government offers 75 per cent of the equipment costs for the radio station, (90 per cent in northeastern states as per order issued on 17th January 2017.

Corporate Social Responsibility (CSR) Funds

Corporate have to spend 2 per cent of their profits for approved schemes under corporate social responsibility. While the broadcasts may not be directly be paid for commercials of company, but community based programs can be sponsored without promoting the corporate through radio programs.

Special funds from Members of Parliament and State Legislature

Every member of Parliament and State Legislature is given a certain fund each year. They have the discretion to spend the same for certain approved schemes. There are examples like Rajya Sabha MP, Dr. Kasturirangan using his funds for infrastructure creation at the radio station run by Myrada at Budhikote, Karnataka.

Key Terms

Sustainability. The process of maintaining broadcasts at a radio station and being able to continuously improve programming.

Revenue. The income to financially sustain the radio station.

Internship. Learn-by-doing methodology for a student.

Micro/nano advertising. Very short advertisements.

7

Understanding the Community Radios of Different Regions in India

Introduction

This chapter shares some successful models of community radio stations in different part of India's North, South, Central, East, and West zones. These examples share the segment that it belongs to--the campus, NGO, or Krishi Vigyan Kendra and the communities they serve. The program formats followed in each station and their respective approach to make it a community participatory radio model are described.

Chapter Structure

- Example from Central India
- Example from North India
- Examples from South India
- Example from Western India
- Example from Eastern India
- Examples of Best Practices

Central India

Chanderi Ki Awaaz

Frequency: 90.4 MHz
Established 27 March, 2010

Total daily transmission: 8 hours (8:00 a.m. to 12:00 p.m., 4:00 p.m. to 8:00 p.m.)

Coverage Area: 15–20 km (sixty to seventy villages)

Program Themes: Promote health and nutrition, rights of women, conservation of local talent, legal awareness, employment, rights, and entitlements.

The journey of *Chanderi Ki Awaaz* began with One World South Asia setting up a community multimedia center in Chanderi with support from UNESCO. The center was created to provide computer and multimedia training to children of the weavers community. Bunker Vikas Sansthan, a local body of weavers' community, submitted an application for the license, and One World South Asia offered capacity building and advisory support on community radio licensing, studio management, and sustained, systematic radio production. Chanderi Ki Awaaz 90.4 MHz was launched on 27 March 2010 in Chanderi, Madhya Pradesh.

Prior to the launch of the community radio station, the organisation was engaged in community radio program production and sharing the programme with the community members through the internet and narrow casting.

Chanderi Ki Awaaz is owned by the community for which it works. The community not only contributed to buy the transmitter but manages it by volunteering to run the station. The station team believes that each community radio must keep its doors and heart open to the needs and ideas of the community to be a true change agent.

Meri Prerna Mera Hunar, a flagship program of *Chanderi Ki Awaaz*, is an ode to the skill building of the rural artisans, especially the weavers of Chanderi who have carved a niche for themselves over a period

Chanderi sarees (long pieces of cloth worn by Indian women) are famous for their unique design. The program helped weavers, who are mostly illiterate, to learn about e-commerce to sell their products online. The program provided a new lease to their business as it helped them use new techniques to market their products not only in their country but worldwide.

The weavers are now getting better prices for their products. This has energized the weavers to take up their business with renewed vigor. The program has taken all the stakeholders of the weaving industry in Chanderi into its fold, which has also facilitated the support of the local handicraft department.

Since the weaving community directly benefited from the program, their participation and sharing of their success has become a learning platform for all those engaged in weaving. The program instilled so much confidence in the minds of the weavers that they overcame their greatest handicap, illiteracy, to embrace e-commerce for selling their products all over the globe. Youth of the target group have shown extraordinary courage to learn, which was initially unthinkable.

North India

Community Radio Alfaz-E-Mewat

Frequency: FM 107.8 MHz

Established 28 February 2012

Total daily transmission: 13 hours

Coverage area: 225 villages in Nuh district, Haryana

Language: Hindi, Mewati, Urdu

Program Themes: Information on agriculture, water, health and sanitation, education, gender equality, women's empowerment, financial literacy, rights and entitlements, entertainment. Folk songs, Kisse Kahani, Participatory. Phone-in Community radio *Alfaz-e-Mewat* FM 107.8 exemplifies an NGO-led model of a radio station. Set up in 2012, the station broadcasts 13 hours on a daily basis reaching to over 225 villages across three blocks of the district.

Since the most essential participants in grassroots development work are local voices, the station broadcasts in the local language in an accessible format to help listeners learn, discuss, and debate important local issues, such as government policies, programs, services, entitlements, agriculture information, and water conservation initiatives. By championing the voices of the most isolated and vulnerable populations, community radio raises citizen awareness and empowers individuals to participate in their own development.

Villagers, schoolchildren, and local artists take an active part in the radio programs. Dozens of community members in Mewat have completed the station's six-month training course, learning how to operate equipment, produce programs, and manage the station as technicians, producers, broadcasters and facilitators. The station's community-based management team has equal representation of women. Programming is designed to encourage female engagement and promote gender equality. Of the thousands of calls the station has received from listeners, nearly 20 per cent have been from women. That number is growing!

The station key programs are *Tohfa-e-Kudrat: Jal, Jangal, Zameen* (gifts of nature: water, forest, and land), *Saaf, Safai aur Sehat* (cleanliness, hygiene, and health), *Kisse Kahani* (local folklore), *Hello Farmaish* (a musical request program), Radio School (tutorials on radio), and others. The station has done series-based programs on governance, financial literacy, mental health and sexual harassment. The linkages the station has managed to build with local government departments such as agriculture, health, education, police and district legal services authorities bring content sustainability.

Alfaz-e-Mewat has been one of the few participating stations trained on the application of Community Learning Program methodology for behavior change, promoted by the Commonwealth of Learning.

Calls received by the station demonstrate that listeners are more aware of entitlements and good practices in water conservation, sanitation, health, education, and agriculture. Villagers are in touch with the needs, aspirations, and views of their neighbors and nearby communities. Awareness campaigns and programs produced at *Alfaz-e-Mewat* are shared with other community radio stations and are available in the public domain on Ek Duniya Anek Awaaz.

The station has won several recognitions including the Manthan award for community broadcasting.

South India

Radio Kotagiri

Frequency: 90.4 MHz

Established 16 February 2013

Total daily transmission: 12 hours (7:00 a.m. to 7:00 p.m.)

Coverage Area: 15–20 km (eighty to ninety villages)

Email: radio@keystone-foundation.org

Program Themes: Folklore and culture, organic agriculture, education, health, conservation

Radio Kotagiri was started on 16 February 2013 to empower the people, particularly the tribal and local communities, and improve the social, environmental, and economic status of the indigenous communities of the Nilgiri Biosphere Reserve by enabling them to find their own voice through the medium of community radio. Radio Kotagiri is managed by members of tribal and indigenous communities in all aspects, from content creation to production and broadcasting to day-to-day running of the radio station operations. A set of trained indigenous people known as (barefoot journalists) play a key role in its success.

Content aired focuses on giving information of importance. The station broadcasts relevant information to build awareness among communities such that they are able to address the issues of the communities that would directly contribute to improve the capacity of the communities to address the issues themselves. The radio programs attempt to utilize resources from within the community (such as village elders, organic farmers, healers, etc.) so that the relevance and acceptance by the people is utmost. Since mobile phones are very common in the area, listeners share feedback through calls and phone-in queries. Feedback is easily obtained from the audience, many of whom may not be able to communicate in writing.

A unique flagship program is *Meri Prerna Mera Hunar* (My inspiration, my skill) that focused on the pottery craft of the Kota community inhabiting the Nilgiris. The Kota is one of the tribal communities that inhabit only seven villages in the Nilgiris, apart from one other. There are two districts in India where this practice is adhered to, and the prevalent one is Nilgiris. The Kotas are an artisan community where pottery is an important part of their annual ritual and the traditional occupation of the Kota people. The program worked from the perspective of reviving the pottery and artisan skills of the community. This craft and industry, only practiced by women, had been on a decline for the past thirty years and many motifs were lost. Pottery is part of their livelihood and a connecting link between other indigenous communities in the Nilgiris.

Connecting people

The program was aired on Radio Kotagiri a number of times and motivated many people to listen and learn about their culture and the importance of pottery. The program gave a larger identity to the artisans, which inspired them look for a larger market to sell their products in more outlets in the town. The community has taken initiatives to revive their artisan skills and market their products in various summer festivals held in the Nilgiris including vegetable shows, fruit shows, etc. The program effectively builds on and brings together the various nuances of pottery from this remote community. The program brought new energy to the skill and to the business as it helped them to use various new platforms to market their products.

Western India

Rudi No Radio

Frequency 90.4 FM

Establishment date 26 November 2009

Total daily transmission: 8 hours

Coverage area: forty villages within a 10-kilometer radius

License holder is Sewa Academy, Thakore Bhai Park, Manipur Village, Taluka Sanand, Dist. Ahmedabad, Gujarat 382110; mahilasewatrust@vsnl.net Program themes: To spread awareness among the listeners, the *Rudi no Radio* team personally visits their areas and organizes training and workshops.

Rudi No Radio was set up in the wake of the Gujarat earthquake in 2000 to act as a medium of communication and source of information and education on social issues. It was the first community radio station exclusively run by women. It has touched many lives as it conducts training and awareness programs on its campus throughout the year. Located inside a training campus, the space is regularly used to connect to people directly. Listeners benefit from the live demonstrations and technical inputs. *Rudi No Radio* focusses on women's empowerment and has set high benchmarks in that it is managed entirely by women from an informal sector.

A Change Harbinger

A flagship program on *Rudi No Radio* called *Satvik Jeevan* emphasizes a healthy and good lifestyle. several times *Rudi No Radio* have organized Satvik food festival for the listeners. One of the listener, Premila ben Patel, participated in the regional food festival organized by the SRISTI. She came with a unique and forgotten dish "pepa ko sabji" . The dish had nutritional and traditional value. She was awarded first prize for her food dish. Another listener, Geeta ben Vaaliya from Chekhla village along with her mother-law started a kitchen garden in the house after listening to a radio program. The family started growing vegetables for self-consumption. Geeta ben's husband, who worked in a private farm, encouraged her,to use cow dung as fertilizer. The surplus crop yield from the kitchen garden is sold to the market that gets them additional income. Although, *Rudi No Radio* is a radio station that run by women and the main focus is women but radio as a medium it is not limited to any specific gender. One of the avid listener Gabhaji thakore, has motivated his daughter- in- law to listen to our programme as it speaks about women growth and empowerment and he bought a radio set for her to encourage her to get good information through *Rudi No Radio*..

Rudi No Radio team creates listener groups to increase the number of listeners and motivate them to contribute information, recipes, music, medicines, etc. The team organizes trainings, workshops, exposure visits, and video replays within community listener groups. The popularity of *Rudi No Radio* is apparent from letters received from listeners demanding regular broadcasts even when there is a programming shift due to a cricket match.

Eastern India

Radio Snehi

Frequency: FM 90.4 MHz

Established: November 17, 2010

Total daily transmission: 18 hours

Coverage Area: 500 villages within a 10–15 KM radius

Licence holder: Snehi Lokotthan Sansthan

Address: Nai Basti Fatehpur, Shivaji Nagar, Siwan, Bihar

Program Theme: Involvement of community members and providing them a multi-dynamic platform for raising various issues.

Snehi Lokotthan Sansthan, a nonprofit, launched *Radio Snehi* as a tool for catering to many unaddressed problems prevailing in the society. *Radio Snehi* invites and encourages local village artists to showcase their talent using the platform of community radio. *Radio Snehi* also engages itself in social development of the community, the station purchases items from local craftsmen and also provides them exhibition halls for showcasing their products. Such activities serve as an additional source of income for the craftsmen and build a strong community connect for the station.

One of the key programs of *Radio Snehi*, *Swayam Swasthya Samuh,* promotes health and hygiene of women and adolescent girls. The station team started to form self-health groups for women and girls. Regular conversation on the topic/issue enabled women leaders to talk further in their self-health groups. The program helped them choose a health topic such as how to maintain hygiene in menstruation. The programs informed the community about health card, roles, and responsibilities of an ANM and ASHA, as well as *anganwadi* workers, health centers, schemes for women and girls' health, nutrition of lactating mothers, pre and post-delivery diet, immunization, benefits of using toilets, consequences/effects on health, going toilets in the open fields, and handwashing. The station team made fifteen different groups of women across villages. In one group, there are ten to twelve women, so 150 women have been engaged with this program.

The self-health groups are famous and many women and girls want to join it. The group stays together for a year. Through this innovation the station team has trained about 300 women and girls. After getting training here, they become health volunteers. They share their learning on radio as well. Most of the women were not aware about the health facilities in their nearby health center. With this program, they came to know about many government schemes on women's health. They built strong groups to talk about their health issues showing the effectiveness of the medium in addressing sensitive issues like menstrual hygiene.

Examples of Best Practices

Community radio creates a wealth of knowledge for listeners. After listening to a radio program, people are inspired to act and adopt more progressive practices. For example, in a radio station *KVK Pravara*, a Science for Women's Health and Nutrition program helped a number of pregnant women who had caesarean operations during their earlier pregnancy. After listening to the series, many of them began eating regular nutritious local foods, went to doctors for reviews, and subsequently had natural births.

Another example is from a radio station *Pasumai* in Tamilnadu, which airs program for the Saurashtra community settled in Dindigul, Tamil Nadu. They are mostly weavers and radio is their stress buster and a companion during their work hours.

Anna CR once organized a training with the Khadi and Village Industries Board on handmade products. The products manufactured were purchased by the university itself.

CR Vasundhara Vahini, Baramati, once aired program for the women workers of the readymade garments group called Cotton kings. Each program diverted the attention of the workers from extraneous things and offered suggestions to increase their productivity while also offering entertainment.

Community participation is ensured by organising various activities for the community at *CMS radio* in Lucknow, Uttar Pradesh. Live phone-in programs, such as *Maati Ke Geet,* are broadcast wherein community members present their requests on the phone to listen to folk songs, and songs are played as per their interest. At times, community members sing folk songs through their phones. They also participate in the drama program, *Rang Manch*. Community members act in plays that are later broadcast through *CMS radio.*

Fisherwomen from R*adio Thendral* Chennai, who were empowered by the station, felt very strongly about their recognition among neighbors and others living nearby. Their husbands recognized their talents. The women have become bold enough to interview doctors on the radio even without a script.

Deccan Radio station in Hyderabad promoted communal harmony by inviting women listeners from diverse religious background.

Radio Active, Bengaluru, set an example by engaging and including the transgender individuals as a part of the radio production team that helped create a space for them to express and be heard.

Yeralavani, Maharashtra provided drought-ridden farmers with an alternative idea cash crop by the name of Dragon fruit.

Shyamalavani, Madurai, provided a platform for Dhanam, who was working as a maid in the primary school, to show her talents, and now she is a well-respected leader in her village, Eliyarpathi, near Madurai.

Waqt Ki Awaaz 91.2 FM, Kanpur came up with the program *Chaukanni Chaar Diwari.* This program spread awareness about the pros and cons of different resources to be used as fuel for cooking.

Radio Mewat partnered with the National Bank for Agriculture and Rural Development for a project on Financial Inclusion in Mewat. The aim of the project was to create awareness and promote financial inclusion of the most vulnerable population in the process of growth.

Geethalakshmi, one who lived in a slum behind *Holy Cross College*, Trichy, became an RJ and later finished her post graduation. She is now heading that station.

An old woman who gave her kitchen to the *Sayere Jo Sangathan* radio station in Kutch, Gujarat, for three years was trained in the operation of equipment and managed the station till the local panchayat offered land, a building, and a restroom for running the station.

A bold woman, Muskan, independently manages the radio station *Muskan* in Phulbani district of Odisha, which is known for its extremist organizations. With the help of small traders in Phulbani, Muskan has been able to maintain her family and also the station.

Hamara MSPICM 90.4 FM, Himachal Pradesh's first community radio, was a venture floated by the M S Panwar Institute of Communication and Management (MSPICM) that was launched in Solan district. The radio content revolves around developmental issues of health, agriculture, employment, government opportunities, literacy programs, and life coping skills, etc., in the local pahadi language.

IIMC and Community Radio

Indian Institute of Mass Communication was one of the earliest applicants for launching community Radio service in the country. The campus situated near Jawaharlal Nehru University, Indian Institute of technology, Qutub Minar, NCERT, and many other important places in the country, has already completed 50 years of its service. It has a very good infrastructure, classrooms, conference halls, auditorium, hostels and guest houses with ample car parking and greenery. The Community Radio station Apna CR 96.9 MHz was launched in 2005 as a campus radio. But it started regular broadcasting only from 2013 as a community radio station. It is now broadcasting seven hours per day. The station boasts of a daily 60 minute phone in Live show 'Apne Aas Pass' to ensure participation of the community nearby. The IIMC has also started paid internships from May 2018. It has association with civil society organizations like Chetna, Society for the Promotion of Youth and Masses, Can Support, Senior Citizens Welfare Association, Centre for Science and Environment, et al. The Institute is now planning to set up Apna Radio CRS in all its campuses including Dhenkanal, Odisha; Amravati, Maharashtra; Kottayam, Kerala, Jammu, Jammu & Kashmir & Aizawl, Mizoram.

The community radio which was broadcasting only for a few hours earlier, got an impetus after the new Director General KG Suresh joined in the year 2016. He envisaged the establishment of a Community Radio Empowerment & Resource Centre, which would impart training to CR professionals and aspirants in content creation, resource management and technology.

The need for a permanent centre for community radio was visualized as early as 2012 when the number or radio stations crossed 150. The community radio facilitation centre with offices at Shastri Bhawan and CEMCA was conceived on the base of this necessity. But it soon lost its identity. The multi ministerial licensing system needed a Facilitation centre. But the need for capacity building was envisaged even before the birth of the first community radio station. The international agencies like UNESCO did facilitate some training programmes using civil society organizations. Indira Gandhi National Open University launched its distance education certificate course . But an institute with a full time course and training was being felt as the major solution to the ailing CR sector. With this in mind the 135th meeting of the Executive council of the IIMC passed a resolution on 18th November 2016 which reads as follows:

The proposal for establishing Community Radio Community Media Empowerment Centre at IIMC was approved by the EC. Members also suggested that before the course is started, various aspects such as feasibility, sustainability, relevancy and content may be examined thoroughly. It was suggested the IIMC can be made as a National Depository of programmes produced by various Community Radio Stations all over the country which can be availed free of cost by the Radio stations. The Community Radio Empowerment & Resource Centre was inaugurated by the then I&B Secretary Shri Ajay Mittal and DG Shri K.G. Suresh on 29 March, 2017.

8

Challenges

Introduction

This chapter shares common challenges faced by a community radio faces. These are categorized by types and include the dilemma of a station having its own identity rather than the entity of the license-holder organization. The challenges of sustainability are not just financial but also include the sustainability of content, regulatory issues, and people.

Chapter Structure

Types of Sustainability

- Content Management Challenges
- Financial Challenges
- Regulatory and Operational Challenges
- Human Resources Challenges
- The Way Forward

Types of Sustainability

A community radio station must walk a tightrope to be able to manage its operations amidst many challenges. The sector which has struggled with various forms of sustainability Since inception still remain a challenge In the dilemma of entity vs. identity, radio stations must not lose sight of the very purpose for which they exist.

Content Management Challenges

- Community radio stations plan their schedules and playlists as envisaged by the station manager and the head of the institution, be it educational, agricultural, or NGO-based.
- Nowhere in the sector is there a regular, functional content management committee.
- Members of the committee are often not selected by a systematic process. They are nominated by the head of the institution after taking suggestions from office bearers, or they are known to them

  No system is in place to regularly update the communication and content needs of the community.
- Community radio stations follow All India Radio, which is information-centric and formal, or commercial radio stations that are mainly entertainment-based and informal. Community radio stations have not found any meaningful alternatives to either of the existing sectors.
- Community radio stations follow the celebrity-based RJ model.
- Systematic volunteer participation in community radio has not been generated or experimented upon.
- Digitalization of frequencies will benefit the sector and make community radio a convergent media. (Frequencies will be available aplenty).
- Many radio stations have not mapped their coverage area primary, secondary, and random.
- Many radio stations do not have their listeners database. The stations did not conduct baseline studies, or they have not saved baseline data if done or know how to make use of that data for sustaining the radio station.
- Many radio stations do not have a landline phone or digital phone-in console.
- Most CR stations do not create an archive, even an offline archive consisting of CDs and pen drives.

- Use of mobile phones for listening and two-way broadcasts, and the use of digital chats such as Facebook audio, WhatsApp audio, and other social media have not been attempted on a large scale by CR stations.
- CR stations often fail to tap the folk arts and music in their areas and create valuable albums.
- Very few CR stations have undertaken road shows, talent-search competitions, health camps, eco camps, etc.
- Very few CR stations have, in the course of three years, followed any drive to involve each family in their listening zone.

Financial Challenges

- Some community radio stations are functional with less than 20,000 rupees a month, and some stations are functional with 200,000 rupees a month. But there is no systematic sharing of various models among community radio stations.
- Community radio stations are not aware of their potential in using their infrastructure and organization for other revenue-earning schemes such as recording audio books and albums and using the office space for other development activities.
- Micro advertising and rural marketing is not known, and trained personnel are not available.
- There is no separate license fee for recorded music to be played by CR stations. The PPL, Film Chambers, and music right holders demand the same amount from CRSs as commercial radio stations.
- CR stations do not have a plan for remunerating the talent or experts, even a nominal amount. Hence retaining talent is an arduous task.

Regulatory and Operational Challenges

- Most stations do not have a clear-cut vision or mission statement.

- The Sammelan of community radio stations organized by the Government (though since kept in abeyance) gives less time to community radio grassroots personnel.
- Though DAVP releases some advertisements after empaneling CR stations, the procedure takes a long time. Of 253 stations, more than 150 are yet to be empaneled.
- State governments fail to understand the value of CR and bar half a dozen states; others do not offer any financial support.
- Governments, international and national funding agencies consider CR stations merely as a propaganda unit.
- Value-added services are not allowed in CR. This means that even live internet streaming is illegal.
- Privately sponsored programs are not allowed. Hence, local business people or establishments cannot sponsor any programs, and programs have to consist of content with spots and jingles.
- There is neither meaningful monitoring of CR stations nor accountability of CR stations. Though they were supposed to have independent bank accounts and send their schedule of programs and audited statement of accounts to the Ministry of Information and Broadcasting, most CR stations do not follow the directive. Even if material is sent, the government doesn't have the machinery to process it.
- A community radio sustenance fund of 100 crores was announced in 2012. After five years, 90 per cent of the money remained unspent. The government increased the subsidy to 75 per cent for new CR stations and 90 per cent to stations situated in the northeast in 2017. At the time of this publication, not much has happened, and the scheme is embroiled in administrative procedures.
- CR institutions in campus establishments typically use it as a status symbol and to get additional points in NAAC ratings. Many NGOs think that community

radio is another project for them. Some CR stations are dysfunctional since the international or national agency which funded them during their initial years stopped further funding.

- Insufficient coordination exists between government departments, particularly from the Ministry of Agriculture.
- The scheme provides powerful transmitters in needy areas, i.e. a 250-watt transmitter instead of the normal 50 watts, but not a single station has been identified to offer this increase in the power of transmission for the past fifteen years.
- There is no tax concession for the equipment in CR stations.
- A community media empowerment center, announced in late 2016, is yet to take off even the foundation plaque had been unveiled.
- No reliable and efficient transmitter for community radio is made in the country. (BEL used to manufacture one and initially offered a lifetime warranty as part of their CSR activities.)
- In most places, the location of the transmitter is not based on the potential reach of the community. Most were not advised properly and hence installed the transmitter and tower in their own buildings. The rules do allow them to select a place, which would give them a higher reach within 15 kms of the area. Some stations selected a nearby hilltop. These stations have good reach and are financially sustainable. Because of the faulty location, signals in some cities and towns do not even reach a 5-km radius.
- While the Ministry of Information and Broadcasting is comparatively quicker to grant letters of intent, the allotment of frequency, SACFA, and WOL from the WPC wing of the Ministry of Telecommunications takes a long time, even years.
- Even if a frequency is allotted, a clash of signals from nearby stations is a problem not solved by computers. In

some cases, commercial radio stations that are very near the frequency of community radio stump the signals with their higher power and height.

- Exposure to policy decisions was never made available to grassroots workers, and the promoters of CR stations are in the same position. All meetings arranged for the sector saw the same people.
- Community Radio Forum, Community Radio Association, and Community radio Federation are the three organizations floated to bring together all the licensees. As of this publication, only Community Radio Association is acting in a truly democratic manner and is recognized by the government.
- Digitalization of frequencies will benefit the sector and make community radio a convergent media.
- The Community Radio Facilitation Center functioning from the Ministry of Information and Broadcasting, and operated by CEMCA with a grant from Ford foundation, became non-functional after a change of leadership.
- Community Radio Facilitation Center, which was considered as a precursor to a one-window concept, could not take off due to objections from the ministries. There are still six stages before getting the final nod.
- Even though ninety days is specified in the guidelines for obtaining the licenses, not a single station in India has been able to get a license within the period. Lack of commitment among the bureaucrats and the will to do so was lacking. No one has been able to predict the time frame and, in some cases, it has taken even five years to obtain a license.
- Some CR stations in locations not reached by any FM signal used their licenses to run a purely commercial channel and broadcasting day-long film songs. The mechanism to punish them is not clear.
- Radio broadcasting can be disrupted due to natural calamities like cyclones, floods, and tsunamis. Once the

antenna or tower is destroyed, it is very difficult to restore them quickly due to financial challenges at the station level and the slow relief grant process at the government level.

Human Resources Challenges

- No formal course or CR training program is available. Some international organizations support training of CR personnel on an ad hoc one-time basis. These trainers concentrate more on the ethics of community radio and community mobilization. There is less practical training. IGNOU launched a six-month certificate course in community radio with practical training at CR stations. CEMCA offered full reimbursement of tuition fees to students. However, after few batches, the course did not attract many takers.
- Given the financial limitations, it is difficult to retain talent including staff and local musicians who perform on radio. There is an ever-floating population in community radio, and people do not consider it a full-time livelihood opportunity as it is a low-pay sector. This means that ongoing capacity building is needed, which again requires funds, which adversely affects the quality of radio programming and the responsiveness to issues and specialized themes that can be addressed through radio.

The Way Forward

Despite all the above-mentioned challenges, community radio has been instrumental in changing the cultural landscape of our nation by being the only mass medium to connect to the grassroots, who often are outside the purview of mainstream media. Since India lives in its villages, this medium had the power to give a platform for many unheard voices, issues, and concerns.

The rich history of evolution of community radio draws its strength from the broadcasting experiments in India and abroad. In its growth trajectory, community radio's journey in India together with the communities has been truly inspiring. The spirit of service that has formed the basis of its evolution places it in a unique position, as community radio has local relevance and importance that mainstream media cannot guarantee. It aspires to inspire communities by disseminating the much-needed information about rights and entitlements, promote local art and culture, preserve local dialects, and enable grassroots heroes to attain a platform for sharing.

As a way forward, the institutional mechanism has to be conducive to give a fillip to this sector to sustain its identity. A few important steps in this direction would be a single window clearance for licensing that can pave the way to a greater number of community radio stations and make it more democratic by allowing stations to broadcast news. Other initiatives include promoting a collaboration mechanism between community and commercial radios, creating a repository of programs for easy access to content on specific themes, and building a cohesive culture that ensures participation and engagement of communities in content development. In addition, there is a pressing need and scope for CR stations to go digital such that their reach is increased. In regard to governance in community radio, it is a skewed picture where there are a lot of responsibilities with little autonomy. The AIR Code of 1967 governs programming on community radio, which is not very positive and provides no guidelines to encourage free and fair debate that reflects diverse opinions on controversial and sensitive matters.

In times where even our national broadcaster under the so-called autonomous Prasar Bharati struggles to find its space and evolve with the changing times, the space for community radio to spread its wings is far less, but it still does exist. It is up to the practitioners and aspirants to work toward thriving this sector amidst the challenges and limitations and turn these challenges into lifelong opportunities engraved in the society.

There is a long way to go for community radio broadcasting and the richness of communities to come fully alive through community radio.

Stay tuned!

References

African Institute for Economic Development and Planning. (2001). *Culture, Communication and Development in Africa.* Retrieved from http://unpan1.un.org/intradoc/groups/public/documents/ IDEP/UNPAN003348.pdf

Agrawal, B. C. (2007). Community radio for women literacy: Insights and lessons from an Indian experiment. *TALEEM Research Foundation.*

Baird, D., Hughes, R., & Nordmann, A. (1998). *Heinrich Hertz.* Dordrecht: Kluwer Academic Publishers.

Bhat. R. et.al. (2017). Working Paper: *Technology & Community Radio.*

CEMCA (2011 & 2012). Strengthening Community Radio in India, A National Consultation.

CEMCA. (2013). Ethical Practice Guidelines for Community Radio Stations. Retrieved from https://cemca.org.in/ckfinder/userfiles/files/Low-Res_EPG_for_CR.pdf

CEMCA. (2014). Innovations in Community Radio: with special reference India. Retrieved from http://www.mib.gov.in/sites/default/files/Innovation_CR_MIB_CEMCA.pdf

Community Radio for Change. (2017). Young India, Namaskar Community Media Network, ActionAid. Retrieved from https://www.actionaidindia.org/wp-content/uploads/2018/06/Community-Radio-for-Change.pdf

Community Radio Policies - UNESCO. (2017). 'Community Media Sustainability Policy Series' Retrieved from https://en.unesco.org/community-media-sustainability/policy-series

Compendium (2014), One World Foundation. Retrieved from http://crfc.in/crs-compendium-2014/

David, M. J. R. (2001). Mahaweli Community Radio. *A Passion for Radio: Radio Waves and Community.*

Deuze, M. (2006). Ethnic media, community media and participatory culture. *Journalism*, *7*(3), 262-280.

Dunaway, D. (1998). Community radio at the beginning of the 21st century: commercialism vs. community power. *Javnost-The Public*, *5*(2), 87-103.

EBU Tech. (1995). *Six great pioneers of wireless.* Retrieved from https://tech.ebu.ch/docs/techreview/trev_263-pioneers.pdf

FAO. (2004). *Communication for Development Roundtable Report: Focus on Sustainable Development*. Retrieved from http://www.fao.org/docrep/008/y5983e/y5983e00.htm

Jankowski, N.W., & Prehn, O. (2002). *Community media in the information age: Perspectives and prospects*. Cresskill, NJ: Hampton Press.

Krüger, F., Monji, R., & Smurthwaite, M. (2013). The healthy community radio station. *Wits Radio Academy and Osisa*.

Kumar K. (2007), 'Community Radio in India: Opportunities and Challenges', Excerpts from the Doctoral Thesis, Educomm Asia, A Quarterly of the Commonwealth Educational Media Centre for Asia, Vol. 12, No. 3, March.

Kumar, K. J. (2000). *Mass communication in India* (Vol. 741). Jaico publishing house.

Likhi, A. (2011). Development Communication in the Digital Era: A Study of Panchayati Raj Institutions and Community Media in Mewat Region of Haryana. Retrieved from http://southasia.oneworld.net/Files/Research%20paper%20synopsis.pdf

Luthra, H. R. (1986). *Indian broadcasting*. Publications Division Ministry of Information & Broadcasting.

Milan, S. (2009). Four steps to community media as a development tool. *Development in Practice*, *19*(4-5), 598-609.

Ngugi PK, Kinyua C (2014) The Concept and Philosophy of Community Radio Stations in the Kenyan Context. J Mass Communicat Journalism 5:233.doi:10.4172/2165-7912.1000233

Pavarala, V., & Malik, K.K. (2007). *Other voices: The struggle for community radio in India*. SAGE Publications India.

Rennie, Ellie (2006-06-28). *Community Media: A Global Introduction (Critical Media Studies)*. Lanham, Md: Rowman & Littlefield.

RIND Survey. July (2018) - Vol. 39. Retrieved from www.pressinstitute.in

Sreedher Ramamurthy, Sundaram KK (2012) Abiding Voices, a study of sustainable radio stations – CEMCA-UNICEF publication. Retrieved from http://cemca.org.in/publicationhome/abiding-voicessustainability-community-radio-india

The One World Network. (2004). Communication for Development-Consultancy report. Retrieved from edaa.in/download/article/C4D.pdf

UNDP. (2006). *Communication for Empowerment-Developing media strategies for vulnerable groups*. Retrieved from https://www.undp.org/content/undp/en/home/librarypage/democratic-governance/civic_engagement/communication-for-empowerment-media-strategies-for-vulnerable-groups.html

UNESCO, 2013. *International comparative survey of community broadcasting regulation*. Retrieved from http://www.unesco.org/new/en/communication-and-information/resources/publications-and-communication-materials/publications/full-list/tuning-into-development-international-comparative-survey-of-community-broadcasting-regulation/

United Nations. (2011). Communication for Development-Strengthening the effectiveness of the United Nations. Retrieved from https://www.undp.org/content/undp/en/home/librarypage/democratic-governance/civic_engagement/c4d-effectivenessofun.html

Venniyoor S. (2006), 'Community Radio Unshackled', Vidura, Journal of the Press Institute of India, Issue: October – December.

Links and Notes

- Ember, Steve, and Shirley Griffith. (2010) The Story of Radio, VOA. https://learningenglish.voanews.com/a/the-story-of-radio--111496664/115991.html

- Wikipedia: https://en.wikipedia.org/wiki/Community_media
- Government Procedure is the biggest hurdle in the growth of Community Radio in India. Retrieved from https://factly.in/community-radio-in-india-government-procedure-is-the-biggest-hurdle-in-the-growth/
- What is Community Radio? World Association of Community Broadcasters. AMARC. http://www.amarc.org/?q=node/47
- Wikipedia: https://en.wikipedia.org/wiki/Gyan_Vani
- MoIB and CEMCA. (2010). A Report on Community Radio Awareness Workshop.

  pib.nic.in/newsite/PrintRelease.aspx?relid=187301
- Certificate Course material from Indira Gandhi National Open University (2008) CCR-BJM 001. *Introduction to Community Radio.*
- Certificate Course material from Indira Gandhi National Open University (2008) CCR-BJM 002. *Introduction to Community Radio.*
- Prabhakar N, (2009). *'A Study on the role of campus radio (Anna FM) in inculcating everyday science awareness among marginalized women'*; thesis report.
- Tamil. S. (2017). *'Trajectories of Community Radio in Tamil Nadu: Ownership, Community Participation and Sustainability'*; thesis report.
- Ujjwala, T. T. & Ramamurthy, S. (2017). *'Measuring Impact of Science Communication Programmes on Women Empowerment through Community Radio'*; thesis report.
- *Compendium on functional community radio stations.* (2013). Retrieved from https://mib.gov.in/sites/default/files/Compendium2013compressed.pdf
- *The History of Radio Technology, Everything You Need to Know About the Invention of Radio*, ThoughtCo. Retrieved from https://www.thoughtco.com/invention-of-radio-1992382

Annexure 1 : Application Process

APPLICATION FORM FOR PERMISSION FOR SETTING UP COMMUNITY RADIO STATION

(Seven Copies to be submitted)

Please log on to www.mib.gov.in for latest policies on community radio before applying for a license

The Secretary,
Ministry of Information & Broadcasting
'A' Wing, Shastri Bhawan,
New Delhi – 110 001

Sir,

I hereby submit the following details in support of the eligibility as prescribed in the guidelines for Grant of permission for setting up Community Radio Station in India.

1. Name of the Institution/Organisation:
2. Location:

   Address Line 1 ....

   Line 2 ....

   Line 3 ....

   City ....

   State ....

   Pin Code ....

(In case of educational institutions, the FM Transmitter and Antenna should be located within the premises of educational institution. In all other cases, the FM Transmitter and Antenna should be located within the geographical area of the community to be served. Please indicate the name of village/town/area etc. where Transmitter & Antenna are to be located and the entire area of service to be covered by the Community Radio along with map). Mobile FM Transmitter and Antenna are not permitted.

3. Mailing Address for Communication:
   Pin Code .... Tel. No. ....
   E-Mail .... FAX ....
4. Local Address, if any (of Delhi).
5. Name of the Head of the Institution/organisation:
6. Name, designation and address of the authorized signatory responsible for complying with the terms and conditions of the Grant of Permission Agreement (GOPA):
   (Details to be furnished as per Annex. II)
7. Details of the organization and members of the Governing Body along with 'Self Declaration': (Please furnish details of members along with bio-data of each member as per Annexure-II)
8. Furnish the following details in case of:

(A) EDUCATIONAL INSTITUTIONS:

(i) Whether the educational institution is government/private or govt. aided:

(ii) Whether recognized by:

  (a) Central Government

  (b) State Government

(Please furnish details along with documentary proof)

(iii) Give a profile of the Institution:

(iv) Details of the Community/Area proposed to be served?

(Enclose an area map indicating the area of service to be covered by the Community Radio)

(v) Please furnish documents (like certificate under section 12-A of Income tax Act or any other document) in support of the institution being "Non Profit" as certified in paragraph 6 of the Certificate/Affidavit (Annexure-I)

(B) AGRICULTURAL UNIVERSITY/ICAR INSTITUTION/KRISHI VIGYAN KENDRA

(i) Whether the Institution/Organisation is private/govt. aided:

(ii) Whether recognized by:

  (a) Central Government

(b) State Government

(Please furnish details along with documentary proof)

(iii) Give a profile of the Institution:

(iv) Details of the Community/Area proposed to be served?

(Enclose an area map indicating the area of service to be covered by the Community Radio)

(C) NON-PROFIT ORGANISATIONS, VOLUNTARY ORGANISATIONS, NGOs ETC.

(i) Whether registered under Societies Act or any other such act relevant to the purpose: (Please furnish details and enclose attested photocopy of the registration certificate)

(ii) Whether completed 3 years of registration at the time of application:

(iii) Enclose a copy of the Memorandum of Article of Association:

(iv) Enclose certified copies of the balance sheet for the last three years of the Organisation/NGO/Civil Society Organisation:

(v) Whether received grant from the Central Govt./State Govt./Multilateral agencies? (if yes, please give details with supporting documents)

Give a profile of the Organisation including past achieve ments, community based projects undertaken.

(vi) Details of the Community / coverage area proposed to be served?

(Also enclose an area map indicating the area of service to be covered by the Community Radio)

(viii) Objective sought to be achieved by setting up the CRS:

OTHER GENERAL INFORMATION TO BE PROVIDED BY ALL APPLICANTS:

9. State the

(i) Power of the FM Radio transmitter:

(Upto 100 watt ERP is generally permitted. In exceptional case, upto 250 Watt ERP could be considered subject to the conditions laid down in the guidelines.)

(ii) Height of the tower:

(Max. 30 meter and Min. 15 meter above the ground level permitted)

10. Location of the FM transmitter & Antenna:
    - (i) Geo-coordinates of the location (in degrees, minutes and seconds):
    - (ii) Height above mean sea level (AMSL in meters):

(In the case of educational institutions, the FM Transmitter and Antenna should be located within the premises of educational institution. In all other cases, the FM Transmitter and Antenna should be located within the geographical area of the community to be served. Please indicate the name of the village/town/area etc. where Transmitter & Antenna is to be located and the entire area of service to be covered by the Community radio along with a map). Mobile FM transmitter and antenna is not permitted.

11. Nature/Types of programmes to be broadcast:
12. Language(s) in which programme is to be produced/broadcast:
13. Number of Hours proposed to be broadcast:
14. Source of content (own/acquired):
15. Profile of the community located in 10 km radius of the institution & their problems:
16. How your programmes are going to help the targeted community:
17. How you propose to involve the local community in the production of programmes and management of CRS:
18. Have you made any survey amongst the community about the need for setting up CRS and the requirements of the targeted population? Give brief details:
19. Details of sources of funding and amount proposed to be invested for –
    - a. Setting up of infrastructure
    - b. Maintenance
    - c. Programme production
20. Foreign Aid, if any:

    (Foreign aid permitted only from multilateral agencies. Please attach a copy of the FCRA clearance.)

21. Details of the processing fee:

Attached Demand Draft No............... dated............ for Rs. 2500/- towards processing fee drawn on

(name of the bank, branch) in favour of Pay & Accounts Officer, Ministry of Information & Broadcasting, New Delhi

(Please note that the DD must be payable at Delhi/New Delhi only)

DECLARATION

i. I/We are duly authorized to sign this application for and on behalf of ____________________ .

ii. I/We hereby certify that the above statements are true and correct to the best of my/our knowledge and belief.

iii. I/We hereby undertake to inform Ministry of Information and Broadcasting if any of the facts furnished above undergo a change in future.

iv. I/We undertake to abide by the programme code of AIR including conditions laid down in para 5 of Guidelines.

v. I/We undertake to preserve tapes/CDs or recordings of the broadcasts in any form for 3 months and provide the same to Government, as and when required.

vi. I/We undertake to comply with all the terms and conditions laid down in the Guidelines and such other instructions as may be issued by the Government from time to time.

vii. Affidavit as in Annexure-I and bio-data of members as in Annexure-II are enclosed.

[Signature of Applicant(s)]

(Name in Block Letters)

Place:
Date:

Designation of Signatory

ANNEXURE -I

CERTIFICATE/AFFIDAVIT

1. I understand that this application, if found incomplete in any respect and/or if found with conditional compliance or not accompanied with the requisite processing fee, shall be summarily rejected.
2. I undertake to follow in letter and spirit the programme code being followed by AIR or any other code(s), which may come into force any time.
3. I understand that if at any time any averments made or information furnished for obtaining the permission is found incorrect, my application shall be liable to be rejected and any permission granted on the basis of this application shall be liable for termination.
4. I certify that the institution/organization shall not undertake transmission of sponsored programmes except the programmes sponsored by Central & State Governments and other organisations to broadcast public interest information.
5. I certify that the institution/organization shall undertake limited advertising and announcements relating to local events, local businesses and services and employment opportunities and the maximum duration of such limited advertising shall not exceed 5 (Five) minutes per hour of broadcast.
6. I certify that the institution/organization is a 'Non-Profit' entity.
7. I certify that the revenue generated from such advertisement and announcements shall be utilized only for the operational expenses and capital expenditure of the CRS. I certify that after meeting the full financial needs of the CRS, surplus amount shall, with prior written permission of the Ministry of Information & Broadcasting, be ploughed into the primary activity of the organization i.e. for education in

case of educational institutions / for furthering the primary objectives for which the NGO has been established.

8. I hereby certify that after issue of Letter of Intent (LOI) by the granter and having obtained the SACFA clearance from WPC wing of Ministry of Communication & IT, I shall sign the Grant of permission agreement (GPOA) for Community Radio Broadcasting with Ministry of Information & Broadcasting. I undertake to comply fully with all the terms and conditions therein; failing which the granter may terminate/revoke/cancel the agreement.
9. I certify that to the best of my knowledge and belief, the statements made in this application are correct. I understand that the Government of India reserves the right to revoke the permission if at any time any statement made is found to be false and to have been made by me or any member or any officer knowing it to be false.

Name and Signature of Authorized Signatory

(Office Seal)

ANNEXURE –II

Self Declaration for Organization and Authorized signatory & All Governing body members/Trustees for whom security clearance is sought.

a. Name & address and registration number of the Organization

b. Name & Addresses of Authorized Signatory & All Governing Body Members/Trustees of the organization (please list)

1.____

2.____

3.____

4.____

5.____

6.____

7.____

....

....

....

....

c. Is the Organization or any of the Governing body members listed above, the subject of any,

1. Preventive detention proceedings (PSA/NSA etc.) : Yes/No
2. Criminal Proceedings : Yes/No
3. Pending Warrants : Yes/No
4. Attachment Proceeding : Yes/No

If, Yes, please provide following details :

1. Detention/case/FIR/Warrant Number :
2. Police Station and District having jurisdiction :
3. Section of law :
4. Name and place of court :

The above mentioned details are in respect of both India and any other foreign country.

Note: The above self declaration is required to be signed and filled by Authorized Signatory of the Organization.

Proforma for furnishing details of Applicant Organization and its authorized signatory & all governing body members/trustees etc.

Details in respect of the Organization/Institutions/Krishi Vigyan Kendra etc.

Full Name of the Organization/ Institution	Date of Registration of the Organization/ Institution	Address of Head Office, Regional Offices and Registered Office	Previcus Name of the Organization, if any	FCRA Registration, if any. If yes, Details of Foreign Contribution Received	Power Output and Height of the Antenna

Details in respect of Authorized Signatory & All Governing Body members/Trustees/Office Bearers etc.

S. No.	Full Name of Board of Directors and Key Executives (Wherever applicable)	Present Position	Date of Birth	Parentage		Present and Permanent Address	Nationality	Passport Nos. and issue date, if any	Contact Address and Telephone Number
				Father	Mother				

(use one row for each member. Add more no. of rows, if required)

Signature of Authorized Signatory & Seal of the Organization

File No. 402/101/2016-CRS

GUIDELINES FOR PROVIDING GRANTS TO COMMUNITY RADIO STATIONS

please refer to www.mib.gov.in for the latest version of the guidelines

New Delhi

Dated: 20th July 2018

Foreword

In July 2013, the Government of India approved a new scheme namely "Supporting Community Radio Movement in India" for providing financial assistance to Community Radio Stations under the component Community Radio Support Scheme (CRSS). The matter has been reconsidered and the Government has now decided to revise the guidelines in terms of eligibility criteria, amount of grant and procedure for release of grant etc. The revised guidelines in this regard are given below:

These guidelines will be applicable to applications for grants for purchase of equipment received since April 2017.

3. Objectives of the scheme:

- Raise awareness about Community Radio (CR) policy guidelines and process involved in establishing of CRS.
- Strengthen infrastructure of both new and existing CR Stations in order to fulfill their community responsibilities.

(B) Capacity building of the prospective and operational CR stations

IV. Promote growth of CRS, especially in remote, rural and poverty stricken areas.

(vi) Promote research & innovations, and learning from each other.

(C) Services:

Grants would broadly cover following areas:

(a) Equipment Acquisition: - capital expenditure for purchase of equipments/up gradation of equipments.

(b) Replacement of existing equipment/ upgradation/ expansion as a one-time cost for existing (on-air) stations.

(c) Emergency Grants: - To cover damages and repairs faced by community radio stations in extreme emergency situations like natural calamities, lightning, cyclone, etc.

(d) Grants for capacity building of operational CRSs and LoI/ GoPA holders.

(e) For awareness generation of CRS policy guidelines and CRS Scheme.

(f) For National and Regional Sammelans, Peer Review and compendium.

GRANT SIZE FOR EQUIPMENT

The maximum grant size for purchase of equipment will be 75% of the total estimated expenditure, subject to a ceiling of Rs. 7.50 lakhs. For North Eastern States (Assam, Arunachal Pradesh, Manipur, Meghalaya, Mizoram, Nagaland, Sikkim & Tripura), LWE and border areas, maximum grant size for purchase of equipment will be to 90% of the total estimated expenditure, subject to a ceiling of Rs. 7.50 Lakhs. The remaining amount will have to be contributed by the grantee.

(D) Eligibility criteria for grant for purchasing equipment by new and existing CRSs:

(i) Any organization which has signed Grant of Permission Agreement (GOPA) with the Ministry of Information and Broadcasting for setting up of Community Radio Station in India, under the extant Guidelines, amended from time to time, will be eligible for grant.

(ii) It will be mandatory that NGOs/Trusts applying for grant/s should be registered on the NGO Darpan Portal of NITI Aayog and have obtained unique ID Number.

(iii) Grants will be provided only for equipment listed by the Ministry. The maximum quantity of each equipment to be considered for grant has also been specified. List of equipment shortlisted and specification/benchmarks thereof are at **Annexure-III.**

(iv) No grant will be provided for land/building/electrical wiring or fixtures, furniture, acoustic treatment and software.

(v) The specifications/benchmarks laid down by the Ministry will be only suggestive and not mandatory for installed equipment. Community Radio Stations will be encouraged to follow the indicative benchmarks for equipment being used for setting up of CRS. However, the use of new technology would be facilitated.

(vi) Equipment purchased after date of allocation of frequency/ Decision to Grant License (D/L) by WPC Wing will only be considered for grant.

(vii) A station will be eligible for grant for a particular equipment only once in 6 years. However, an applicant may make applications for different equipment at different times. The maximum grant in one or more attempts will be restricted to Rs. 7.5 Lakhs. Stations which have already received grant under the scheme will not be eligible to re-apply for the equipment already supported.

(E) How to apply for Grant for purchased equipment:

(i) No prior approval for release of grant is required from Ministry of Information and Broadcasting. The eligible organizations would be required to apply for release of grant, in the prescribed format, after setting up CRS and operationalising it for 3 months. Prescribed format are at **Annexure: I**.

(ii) Already operational stations may apply for release of grant immediately after purchasing and installation of equipment.

(iii) After receipt of application for release of grant, field visit of the operational station will be done by PMU or a person deputed by the Ministry. The inspecting officers will submit their reports to the Ministry in the format prescribed by the Ministry with list of equipment/facilities set up and its operationalisation status. Field Visit Format is at Annexure: II.

(iv) The grant will be released after submission of field visit report with the approval of Joint Secretary, I & B.

2

(vii) Priority will be given to:

- Applicants from North-East Region.
- Applicants who have not received any grant in the past, or are not presently receiving Government grants/public funds for the setting up and/or running of the Community Radio Station. If an applicant has access to or has availed public funds for the same purpose (CR), then the applicant automatically gets de-prioritised.
- Applicants from backward districts (Refer BRGF List)
- Applicants from LWE districts.

(ix) All grantees which have got assistance under the equipment acquisition and replacement will need to go through a **cool-off Period of 6 years** before they can reapply for same equipment. However such grantees can apply for other categories.

10. Emergency Grants:

- Emergency Grants will be provided to CRS in extreme emergency situations only like natural calamities, lightning, cyclone, etc. to cover damages caused to CR Stations. It will be only for equipment replacement. In case of damages during natural calamities, applicant will intimate the Ministry with list of equipment damaged and cause. Damages will be certified by nearest All India Radio/Doordarshan station or any organization/person authorized by the Ministry to do so and a report will be submitted to the Ministry.
- The Secretary I & B shall be the final authority to decide whether to treat a case under emergency grants. The maximum limit for emergency grants will also be Rs. 7.5 Lakhs, with 100% grant.
- The process of release of grant will be same as prescribed for new/operational CRS.

11. Funds for capacity building of LOI/GOPA holders and existing CRSs:

As part of capacity building process, a Training Need Assessment (TNA) was conducted amongst operational Community Radio Stations. Total 62 operating CR stations had given their inputs on TNA format.

From TNA, it was found that there are several key areas on which capacity building is required were identified, which are as follows:

11. Sustainability: Financial, technical, content, human resource and community engagement
20. Content development by community
21. CR Policy Guidelines
22. Code of Ethics
23. Operations and Maintenance

 To discuss the findings of TNA with stakeholders a meeting was invited in July 2015. In the meeting, it was decided that capacity building on above mentioned themes may be conducted. In the meeting, it was also decided that an RFP on capacity building would be floated and theme wise proposals may be invited.

 The expenditure on capacity building would also have positive impact on other components of the scheme. It is envisaged that through capacity building, the existing CRSs, GOPA holders and LOI holders would be in a better position to decide about purchase of equipment, setting up of infrastructure, content production, community engagement and sustainability etc. This will lead to

3

increase in strike rate of operationalisation of CRS and hence more number of application for grants for purchase of equipment and innovations.

19. Implementation of the Scheme's Various Activities

Scheme will be implemented by existing PMU in the Ministry.

PMU will administer the grant making process and will be responsible for:

- Setting up and maintaining of a transparent and accountable administration system
- Announcing and publicizing the Scheme
- Drafting and documenting operating procedures for the Scheme
- Implement the recommendations
- Tracking progress of grants and managing the progress reports
- Undertaking field visits for inspection of purchased equipment and for various other activities
- Visits stations to check whether stations are broadcasting as per CRS policy guidelines
- M&E evaluation activities and
- Any other tasks assigned by the Ministry

22. Year wise and activity wise proposed costing for scheme: (valid upto 2019-2020)

(In Rs. Crores)

S. No.	Activity	Proposed Expenditure		Grand Total
		2018-19	2019-20	
1	Admin. Expenses	0.75	0.75	1.50
2	Grants for equipment purchase including Emergency grants	6.00	6.00	12.00
3	Grants for Capacity Building	3.06	3.06	6.12
4	08 awareness workshops (40 participants/ workshop	0.80	0.80	1.60
5	02 Regional Sammelans of operational CRSs	0.50	0.50	1.00

6	01 National Sammelan/ Exhibition for operational CRS	0.60	0.60	1.20
7	Printing of CRS Compendium	0.10	0.10	0.20
8	Presentation of National CR Awards.	0.05	0.05	0.10
9	Peer review of CRSs.	0.50	0.50	1.00
10	Study on effectiveness of CRS	0.05	0.00	0.05
11	Grant for new research/study/ evaluation		0.23	0.23
	Total Amount			**25.00**

4

13. Other Conditions of the Scheme:

10. The assets will be held in the premises and books of accounts of the grantee. The maintenance of such assets will be done by concerned CRS station. Physical assets acquired wholly or substantially through grant shall not be disposed off/ declared obsolete and unserviceable or condemned before 5 years of purchase. The grantee shall be required to adhere to provisions laid down in GFR while disposing of equipment/ declaring obsolete and unserviceable. The transmitter shall be disposed off by grantee as per procedure laid down by WPC Wing of Department of Telecommunication.
11. Applicants must conform to pre-agreed timelines, both in terms of application and utilization of the grant and ensure that utilization of grants are commensurate and conform to their purpose. Also applicant will maintain transparent and auditable financial records of the grant and its utilization.
12. Failure to comply with the grant regulations specified, or with other reporting or procedural process prescribed, may invite punitive clauses which may escalate up to full revocation of the grant, and recovery of funds disbursed as part of the grant, or assets created out of the grant.

13. Conditions which may invite application of such punitive clauses may include (but are not limited to):
    - The grant not being used for the specific purposes it was granted for;
    - The non-maintenance of appropriate financial records or documentation;
14. Punitive actions may include blacklisting by the CRSS; the recommendation to various ministries of the Government of India and other donor agencies for such blacklisting; and the initiation of legal action in order to force grant compliance or asset/funds recovery.

****

5

Application for Release of Grant for Purchased Equipment for Community Radio Station under the Scheme "Supporting Community Radio Movement in India"

The Secretary,
Ministry of Information & Broadcasting
'A' Wing, Shastri Bhawan,
New Delhi – 110 001

Subject: Application for release of grant for purchasing equipment for Community Radio Station.

Sir,

I/we hereby submit following details to release grant for purchasing equipment for Community Radio Station under the scheme "Supporting Community Radio Movement in India".

c. Name of the Institution/Organisation:
d. Name of Community Radio Station:
e. Date of operationalisation of station:
(Enclose a copy of Wireless Operating License)

f. Complete Address of location of Community Radio Station:
   Address Line 1 ....
   Line 2 ....
   City ....
   State ....
   Pin Code ....
   Tel. No.............................., Mob:.................................,
   E-Mail ....

g. Address for Correspondence:
   Address Line 1 ....
   Line 2 ....
   City ....
   State ....
   Pin Code ....
   Tel. No. ...., Mob: ....,
   E-Mail ....

h. Name of the Head/contact person of the Institution/organisation/CRS:

i. Unique I.D. No. of NGO Darpan Portal of NITI Ayog *(for NGO/Society/Trusts/Voluntary organisations)*

   (In case you do not have unique ID, please register on NGO Darpan Portal of NITI Ayog at: http://ngo.india.gov.in/auth/default.php

d. Details of equipment purchased and installed:

   (Please fill up the details in prescribed format i.e Annexure-1I)

e. Total cost of equipment purchased and installed:

f. (i) Have you received grant from any other source to Purchase Equipment for Community Radio.

3. If yes, please provide details of equipment purchased (Name of equipment, make & model)

   Name of Equipment Purchased:

   (Please attached list of equipment purchased in a separate sheet)

11. Details of Bank Account in which grant is to be transferred:
    (i) Name of account holder: ....
    (ii) Name & address of Bank: ....
    (iii) Account No: ....
    (iv) IFSC Code: ....
    (Pl. attach a copy of cancelled cheque of the account)

Signature of Authorized Signatory

12. Declaration:

I hereby undertake that the information provided in the application and annexures is true to the best of my knowledge. I understand that if at any time any averments made or information furnished for obtaining the grant is found incorrect, the grant provided on the basis of this application shall be liable to be recovered.

Signature of Authorized Signatory

(Name & Designation)

Date:
Place:

Office Seal

Check list of documents to be attached with application:

(i) Details of equipment purchased and installed.
(ii) Copy of Wireless Operating License from WPC Wing.
(iii) Original invoice (s) of equipment purchased and installed.
(iv) CDs in MP 3 format of content broadcasts by CRS in last 3 months (for new CRS only).
(v) No duplicate grant certificate.

Performa for field inspection of Community Radio Station for the purpose of release of grant for equipment

1. Name of Visiting officer: ....
   Telephone/mobile No: ....
   E-mail:..
2. Designation:..
3. Name and address of Department to which officer belongs:
   Address Line 1 ....
   Line 2 ....
   City ....
   State ....
   Pin Code ....
4. Name and address of Community Radio Station visited:
   Address Line 1 ....
   Line 2 ....
   City ....
   State ....
   Pin Code ....
5. Date of visit of station:
6. Details of equipment installed in stations: (in the format annexed)
7. Total cost of installed equipment:
8. Over all status/condition of station:
9. Any other information, if any:

Signature of the visiting officer

(Name and Designation)

Date:
Place:

List of CRS equipment for which grants will be provided and their suggested bench marks

S.N.	Name of equipment	Maximum Quantity to be considered for grant
1	50 W FM (CRS) Transmitter (Conforming to ITU norms for operation between 87.0 Mhz to 108 Mhz)	2 (Single or 1+1 configuration with rack)
2	Self Supported Transmission tower/ Guyed wire Transmission tower/Concrete Transmission tower up to 30 meter	01
3	2 bay, vertically polarized (Omni Directional) VHF Transmitting Antenna conforming to WPC regulation	01
4	Low loss RF Cable with N connector on both ends	01
5	Off Air Monitoring set up/ Logger	01
6	Monitor, 50 W	01
7	8 Channel on-air Broadcast console	02
8	Dynamic cardioids/condenser Microphones	06
9	Portable solid state field recorders	08
10	Headphones	08
11	Personal computers (one with on air recording/automation software)	05

12	2 channel sound card with differential input	05
13	3 KVA, 3 phase or single phase input online UPS with 30 minutes back up	01
14	Phone in equipment	01
15	3 KVA generator set/Solar Power Generator	01
16	Split air conditioners, 0.5 ton to 1.5 ton -2 Nos	02
17	Audio Processor	01
18	50 Watts Dummy Load, matching transmitter Specifications	01

Note: The quantity mentioned against each equipment is maximum, which may be considered for grant. However, Stations may purchase lessor quantity of any equipment, as per their budget.

Annexure 2 : Sample Questionnaire

Sample BASELINE SURVEY- theme based
SCIENCE FOR WOMEN – HEALTH AND NUTRITION

Adapted from the project catalysed and supported by Department of Science and Technology, Government of India- with aknowledgements to Commonwealth of Learning

Respondent Number **City Code**

PART A: MEDIA PROFILE

Media Ownership	Yes	No	Names Of NP/MAGS
1. Do you receive a newspaper at home	❐ 1.	❐ 2.	
2. Do you receive magazines at home	❐ 1.	❐ 2.	
3. Do you own a TV set?	❐ 1.	❐ 2.	
4. If yes, do you have a cable /DTH	❐ 1.	❐ 2.	
5. Does your radio set has FM Band?	❐ 1.	❐ 2.	

7. **Do you listen to radio?** ❐ Yes ❐ No
8. **If Yes, how, (or on what gadget) do you usually listen to radio?**

❐ 1.	Radio set	PLEASE NOTE : IF RESPONDENT DOES NOT LISTEN TO RADIO, SKIP REMAINING QUESTIONS AND GO TO SECTION B
❐ 2.	Mobile phone	
❐ 3.	Music system	
❐ 4.	Car stereo	
❐ 5.	Other (specify) ____________	
❐ 6.	DO NOT LISTEN	

9. Where do usually listen to radio?

<table>
<tr><td>❒ 1.</td><td>At home</td><td rowspan="6">PLEASE NOTE :
IF RESPONDENT DOES NOT LISTEN TO RADIO, SKIP REMAINING QUESTIONS AND GO TO SECTION B</td></tr>
<tr><td>❒ 2.</td><td>In the car while driving</td></tr>
<tr><td>❒ 3.</td><td>At neighbour's/ friend's house</td></tr>
<tr><td>❒ 4.</td><td>At meetings:group/ community listening</td></tr>
<tr><td>❒ 5.</td><td>Other (specify)
____________________</td></tr>
<tr><td>❒ 6.</td><td>DO NOT LISTEN</td></tr>
</table>

10. How often do you listen to the radio? (*Tick one*)

❒ 1. Regularly (6-7 times a week)	❒ 4. Rarely (once a week or less)
❒ 2. Frequently (4-5 times a week)	❒ 5. **Do not listen (GO TO SECTION B)**
❒ 3. Occasionally (2-3 times a week)	

11. When do you usually listen to Radio? *(Tick as many as applicable)*

❒ 1. 6-8 AM	❒ 5. 3-5 PM
❒ 2. 8-10 AM	❒ 6. 5-8 PM
❒ 3. 10-1 PM	❒ 7. 8-10 PM
❒ 4. 1-3 PM	❒ 8. after 10 PM

12. For how long do you listen to radio (total duration per week) in a week?

❒ Less than an hour ❒ 1-4 hours ❒ 4-8 hours

❒ More than 8 hours

13. What channels do you listen to most?

❒ 1. All India Radio ❒ 2. Commercial FM

❒ 3. CRS (eg. Radio Snehi)

14. Can you list out the CRSs in your locality/region?

(Note down responses. Do not prompt)

1.______________________________
2.______________________________
3.______________________________

15. Have you heard of your CRS (eg. Radio Snehi)?
❒ 1. Yes ❒ 2. No

(INSTRUCTION: IF YES, ASK QUESTION 12-17)

16. Have you ever heard any programmes on your CRS
❒ 1. Yes ❒ 2. No

17. When did you last listen to your CRS / Radio Snehi? *(Tick one)*

❒ 1. Today	❒ 4. Few days ago
❒ 2. Yesterday	❒ 5. Cannot remember
❒ 3. Two days ago	❒ 6. Have not heard of your CRS

18. Which programme was that?
(You may get responses to one or all three of the sub-questions. From one of the responses, the other two can be deciphered).
❒ 1. Programme name ______________
❒ 2. Programme Type (Music/Talk show/drama, etc.)
____
❒ 3. Programme slot ______________
❒ 4. Not applicable (if response to Q 17 is 5 or 6)

19. What do you like most about your CRS Channel? *(Tick up to 3 items)*
Do not read out the list. Tick the most appropriate option, as per response)

❒ 1. I get useful information
❒ 2. I get to hear about new things happening in my neighbourhood
❒ 3. I get to hear voices of my community
❒ 4. I like the programmes
❒ 5. I like the music

❒ 6. I can participate in the programmes
❒ 7. I like the presentation style
❒ 8. I get useful information on health
❒ 9. Others: specify ________________
❒ 10. DO NOT LISTEN

20. Have you ever participated in any programme on CRS?

❒ 1. Yes ❒ 2. No

21. If yes, please indicate how you have participated (*Tick as many as applicable)*

❒ 1. CRS events (competitions/medical camps etc)
❒ 2. Phone-in programmes
❒ 3. Discussions held by CRS
❒ 4. In programme production (idea, script, recording)
❒ 5. As talent (voice, music ETC)
❒ 6. Any Other: Specify
❒ 7. HAVE NOT PARTICIPATED

22. Can you name some programmes you have liked on CRS?

Write name in Column 1. Select codes for Time and Type and enter in Columns 2 and 3

Name (Name of the programme)	Time (code)	Type (code)
1.		
2.		
3.		

Name of the Programme	Time codes		Program Types	
INSTRUCTION: LIST NAMES OF 10-12 PROGRAMS THAT ARE BROADCASTED ON YOUR CRS	❐ 1. 6- 8 AM	INSTRUCTION: ONCE RESPONDENT MENTIONS A PROG. ASCERTAIN THE TIME AND ENTER TIME CODE IN COLUMN 2	❐ 1. Music	INSTRUCTION: ONCE RESPONDENT MENTIONS A PROG. ASCERTAIN THE TYPE AND ENTER PROG TYPE CODE IN COLUMN 3
	❐ 2.. 8-10 AM		❐ 2. Drama	
	❐ 3. 10- 1 PM		❐ 3. Feature	
	❐ 4. 1-3 PM		❐ 4. Phone in	
	❐ 5 .3-5 PM		❐ 5 . Interviews	
	❐ 6. 5-8 PM		❐ 6. Talk show	
	❐ 7. 8-10 PM		❐ 7. Quiz	
	❐ 8. After 10 PM		❐ 8.Others	
	❐ 9. Varies, no fixed time			

PART B: HEALTH RELATED ISSUES

23. What do you do when you or someone in the family falls ill?

(Response may be more than one)

❐ 1. Visit Govt. hospital/ PHC/CHC
❐ 2. Visit a private doctor/clinic
❐ 3. Follow traditional medicine remedies on my own
❐ 4. Visit faith healer
❐ 5. Visit alternate healer
❐ 6. Follow a home-based remedy
❐ 7. Other (specify) ________________

24. What is your primary source of information regarding the following issues?

Note: Tick any one of the following options.

Topic	1 = Newspaper	2 = TV	3= Radio	4= Friends/ relatives	5 = Doctors/ Health workers	6 = Others
1. Child welfare						
2. Nutritious Health care for family						
3. Personal well being						
4. General family Health						
5. Healthy practices for prevention of diseases						

6. Pregnancy – care/ precautions						
7. Young adult Health care and welfare						
8. Health care and welfare of elderly						

25. Have you or your family members suffered from any serious illness? Specify.

❒ 1. No ❒ 2. Yes (Specify. Responses may be more than one)

____

❒ 2a. How did you treat it?

____

26. Do you know about diarrhoea? ❒ 1. No ❒ 2. Yes

❒ 2a. If yes, do you know how to treat it? (Note down response)

____

27. Do you what is Tetanus? ❒ 1. No ❒ 2. Yes

❒ 2a. If yes, how can it be prevented? (Note down response)

____

28. Do you know about Anaemia (iron deficiency)?

❒ 1. No ❒ 2. Yes

❒ 2a. If yes, how how should it be treated? (Note down response)

____

29. In case of a trauma, or injury to yourself or someone in the family, how would you treat it? *(Note down response)*

____

30. Do you know about worm infestation? ❒ 1. No ❒ 2. Yes

❒ 2a. If yes, how should it be treated? (Note down response)

____

31. Have you heard about HIV/AIDS? ❑ 1. No ❑ 2. Yes
❑ 2a. If yes, what was your source of information? (Note down response)

____

MOTHER AND CHILD RELATED ISSUES *(To be administered to mothers only)*

32. Care during pregnancy

What kind of care did you take during pregnancy? *(Tick as many as applicable)*

(Do not read out the options. Tick as per response.)

❑ 1. I took IFA tablets
❑ 2. I went for periodic check-ups
❑ 3. I followed a more nutritious diet than before
❑ 4. I took more rest than otherwise
❑ 5. I did not change my lifestyle in any particular way
❑ 6. Others (specify) ______________________________

____

Delivery

33. Where did you have your delivery?
❑ 1. Institutional (Hospital/ PHC/CHC)
❑ 2. At home

34. Who handled your delivery?
❑ 1. Doctor ❑ 2. Nurse ❑ 3. ANM ❑ 4. Dai
❑ 5. ASHA worker ❑ 6. Other (Specify) ________________

35. Has your child/children been vaccinated? ❑ 1. Yes ❑ 2. No
❑ 2a. If no, what were the reasons for not vaccinating?

____

36. Have you breast-fed the child/children? ❑ 1. Yes ❑ 2. No
❑ 2a. If yes, for how long?) _________________________

37. What kind of post-partum care did you receive? *(Note down response)*

____

38. Can you share with us some of the common beliefs and practices related to pregnancy, especially with regard to food?

____

____

____

FOOD AND NUTRITION

39. What is your source of drinking water?

❒ 1. Private tap ❒ 2. Pond/lake ❒ 3. Private well

❒ 4 Common tap/well ❒ 5. Handpump/borewell

40. Is it potable? ❒ 1. Yes ❒ 2. No

42. If no, how do you treat it to make it potable?

❒ 1. Boil ❒ 2. Water filter

❒ 3. Other (Specify) ______________________________

43. Where do you get your fruits and vegetables from?

❒ 1. Own garden ❒ 2.Market

❒ 3. Others (specify) ______________________________

44. Are you aware of / have access to PDS (ration shops) in your locality? ❒ 1. Yes ❒ 2. No

45. Do you know how to select fruits and vegetables?

❒ 1. Yes ❒ 2. No

46. Are you aware of locally available fruits and vegetables?

❒ 1. Yes ❒ 2. No

47. Are you aware of adulteration in spices and cereals?

❒ 1. Yes ❒ 2. No

48. Can you tell us briefly, about the kind of food you eat?

Breakfast ______________________________

Lunch ______________________________

Dinner ______________________________

CR related

49. Do you have any ideas on how the CR can play a better role for the community?

____

50. Given the opportunity, would you like to participate in Radio Programme?

❒ 1. Yes. ❒ 2. No ❒ 3. Not sure.

51. If basic training is provided, would you like to be a Radio Jockey/Announcer?

❒ 1. Yes. ❒ 2. No ❒ 3. Not sure.

52. Would you like to listen to programme in a group with others listeners?

(Briefly Explain the Idea of a Listener's Club)

❒ 1. Yes. ❒ 2. No ❒ 3. Not sure.

PART C: SOCIO-DEMOGRAPHIC PROFILE OF RESPONDENT

Name of the Respondent:	**Age** (in completed years)
53. Address	
54. Do you have a landline phone: ❒ 1.Yes ❒ 2. No If yes, Number: ________________	
55. Do you have a mobile phone: ❒ 1.Yes ❒ 2. No If yes, Number: ________________	
56. Does anyone else in the Family have a mobile phone? ❒ 1. Yes. ❒ 2. No If yes, Relationship: ________________	
57. Respondent's Marital Status (*Tick one)* ❒ 1. Unmarried ❒ 2. Married ❒ 3. Divorced/Separated ❒ 4. Widowed	

58. Education of the respondent: ***(Tick Only One)***	**59. Occupation of the respondent:*(Tick Only One)***
❒ 1. Illiterate	❒ 1. Wage labourer
❒ 2. Literate but no formal education	❒ 2. Skilled worker
❒ 3. School up to 5 years (Class1-5)	❒ 3. Petty Trader(shop keeper)
❒ 4. School up to 6-9 years (Class 6-9)	❒ 4. Self employed
❒ 5. SSC/HSC	❒ 5. Service – Government
❒ 6. Under Graduate	❒ 6. Service Private
❒ 7. Graduate /Post Graduate (General)	❒ 7. Homemaker
❒ 8. Professional (Doctor, Engg, LLB, MBA)	❒ 8. Student
❒ 9. Technical (Diploma/IT)	❒ 9. Retired
❒ 10. Others (Specify) ________________	❒ 10. Others

60. Currently how many persons live in this House?

____

61. How many children? ______________________________

62. Are the children (of school-going age) attending school?

❒ 1. Yes ❒ 2. No

Class and school ________________________

63. Who is the Head of the Household?	**64. Where does the male head of the house Live?**
❒ 1. Female:	❒ 1. In this village /city
❒ 2. Male:	❒ 2. Outside this village/city
	❒ 3. Outside the country
	❒ 4. No male household head

65. Does the house have electricity? INSTRUCTION: OBSERVE AND WRITE
❒ 1. Yes ❒ 2. No

<table>
<tr><td colspan="2">66. Type of House INSTRUCTION: OBSERVE AND WRITE
❒ 1. Hut
❒ 2. Semi Pucca/Thatched roof
❒ 3. Pucca
❒ 4. Apartment
❒ 5. Independent house/Bungalow
❒ 6. Others: (specify): ________________</td></tr>
<tr><td>67. What type of cooking fuel do you use (Tick as many Applicable)
❒ 1. LPG/Gas
❒ 2. Kerosene
❒ 3. Firewood
❒ 4. Gobar gas/bio fuels
❒ 5. Others: Specify:
________</td><td>68. What toilet arrangements do you have?
(Tick only one)
❒ 1. Private (in your own house)
❒ 2. Common (shared by others)
❒ 3. Open fields
❒ 4. Others: Specify: ________</td></tr>
<tr><td>69. Are there any persons with disabilities in the house?
❒ 1. Yes ❒ 2. No</td><td>70. If yes, state nature of disability:
❒ 1. Visual
❒ 2. Hearing/speech
❒ 3. Orthopaedic
❒ 4. Mental</td></tr>
<tr><td>71. Currently are you member of a Self Help Group?
❒ 1. Yes ❒ 2. No
If yes, DETAILS:
❒ 5. 6001-7500
❒ 6. 7501-9000
❒ 7. 9001-10500
❒ 8. Above 10500</td><td>72. Currently are you a member of any social group, association etc.?
❒ 1. Yes ❒ 2. No
If yes, DETAILS:
❒ 5. Air cooler
❒ 6. Washing Machine
❒ 7. Car/jeep
❒ 8. Computer</td></tr>
</table>

❒ 9 Do not know/ Do not want to say	❒ 9. Air conditioner ❒ 10. Cycle ❒ 11. Other (specify) ________
73. Indicate your monthly Household Income ***Instruction: Tick Only One*** ❒ 1. up to 1500 ❒ 2. 1501-3000 ❒ 3. 3001-4500 ❒ 4. 4501-6000	**74. Assets owned by the Household** ***Instruction: Tick As Applicable*** ❒ 1. Tape Recorder ❒ 2. CD Player ❒ 3. Motorcycle ❒ 4. Electric Mixer/Grinder/ Food Processor

Name of the investigator: **Name of the supervisor:**

Questionnaire credits:

Sreedher Ramamurthy, Shirley Deepak and Alexis Carr, R. Balasubramanian, Commonwealth of Learning – Impact assessment 2017

Annexure 3 : List of Community Radio Stations in India (State/Location wise) (Source: Community Ratio Association)

Frequencies: 90.4, 90.7, 90.8, 91.2, 96.9, 106.8, 107.2, 107.4, 107.8 MHz : Power 50 watts VU2JOS 3 Dec 18

No.	State	Location	MHz	Station	Contact details	Languages of broadcast
1	Andhra Pradesh	Bhimavaram	90.4	Radio Vishnu	Tel:08816-250856, 96668 32284 radiovishnu@gmail.com	Telugu, Hindi, English
2		Chittoor	90.4	Karshaka Vani	pmvrs2002@gmail.com	Telugu
3		Guntur	91.2	ANU Radio	Acharya Nagarjuna University, Nagarjuna Nagar, Guntur. www.nagarjunauniversity.ac.in	
4		Kakinada	90.8	Radio Ala	Tel: 77949 82345, 92480 40968. radioala90.8fm@gmail.com	Telugu
5		Srikakulam	90.4	GMR IT FM	Tel: 08941-252686, 94417 08119 community.radio@gmrit.org	Telugu, English
6		Tirupati	90.4	SVFM CRS	Tel: 0877-2264055, 98662 34482 vibhishanasarma2008@yahoo. co.in	Telugu, Hindi, English
7	Arunachal Pradesh	Itanagar	90.8	Radio City	Tel: 94368 96558 info@tarhuksamaj.org	

8	Assam	Dibrugarh	90.4	Radio Brahmaputra	Tel: 0373-2303584 contactradiobrahmaputra@gmail.	Assamese, Chadri, Bhojpuri, Bodo, Mishing,
9		Guwahati	90.4	Jnan Taranga	Tel: 0361-2235971, 1800 3453613 kkh_sou@yahoo.com	Assamese, Hindi, English, Bengali, Boro, Nepali, Karbi
10		Guwahati	90.8	Radio Luit	Tel:0361-2673728 92074 10112 radioluit@gmail.com	Assamese, Bengali, Hindi, Bodo, Nepali, English
11	Bihar	Bhagalpur	90.4	Radio Active	Tel: 0641-2620183 radioactivebhagalpur@gmail.com	Bhojpuri, Hindi, English, Angika
12		Chapra	90.8	Radio Mayur	Tel: 8587036060, 06152-242908 mayurkalakendra@gmail.com	Bhojpuri, Hindi
13		Gopalganj	90.4	Radio Rimjhim	Tel: 99340 76913 radio_rimjhim@yahoo.co.in	Hindi, Bhojpuri
14		Patna	90.4	Uttam Radio	Tel: 0612-3269706, 98350 20036 uksingh@zhi.org.in	Hindi
15		Patna	91.2	KVK	Tel: 0641-2452611 patnakvk@gmail.com	Hindi, Bhojpuri

16		Samastipur		KVK	Krishi Vignan Kendra, Birauli, Samastipur	
17		Siwan	90.4	Radio Snehi	Tel: 06154-228276, 93340 69148 snehingo@rediffmail.com	Bhojpuri, Hindi
18	Chandigarh	Chandigarh	90.4	Vivek FM	Tel: 0172-2698988/2699428 vivekfm@gmail.com	Punjabi, Hindi, English
19		Chandigarh	91.2	Jyothirgamaya	Tel: 98150 09753 purradio@gmail.com	Punjabi, Hindi, English
20		Chandigarh	107.8	Desh Bhagat Radio	Tel: 97807 77733 deshbhagatradio@gmail.com	Punjabi, Hindi, English
21	Chhatisgarh	Bilaspur	90.4	Raman Radio	radioraman653@gmail.com	Chhattisgarhi, Hindi
22		Raipur	90.4	Radio IGKV	Tel: 0771-2442672 surendratuteja@gmail.com	Chhatisgarhi, Hindi
23		Raipur	90.8	Samvad Radio	Tel: 94257 55699 drnarendra88@gmail.com	Chhatisgarhi, Hindi
24		Surguja	90.4	Radio Neotech	Tel: 94252 54338 neotechtimes@gmail.com	Hindi, Surgujiha, English
25	Delhi	New Delhi	90.4	DU 90.4 FM (Off Air)	Tel: 011-2766 7600 dufm90.4@gmail.com	Hindi, English
26		New Delhi	90.4	Radio JIMS	Tel: 011-40619200 radio.vk@jagannath.org	Hindi, English

27		New Delhi	90.4	Radio Jamia	Tel: 011-26981717 www.jmi.ac.in/jcr	Urdu
28		New Delhi	90.8	KRIMS FM	Tel: 011-47529008 krimsneerajkaran@gmail.com	Hindi
29		New Delhi	96.9	Apna Radio	Tel: 011-26741542 chari.raghav@gmail.com	Hindi, English
30		New Delhi	96.9	JIMS Community Radio	Tel: 011-45184106, 98103 29244 jimscr96.9@gmail.com	Hindi, English
31	Gujarat	Ahmedabad	90.4	Micavaani	Tel: 89800 30745 tarang10@micamail.in	Gujarati, Hindi, English
32		Ahmedabad	90.4	Rudi No Radio	Tel: 98254 15062, 079-26577115 sewaacdy@youtele.com	Gujarati
33		Ahmedabad	90.8	Guruvani	Tel: 079-26302409 www.gujaratuniversity.ac.in/	Gujarati, Hindi, English
34		Ahmedabad	107.8	Radio Nazariya	Tel: 079-25601660, 74900 38283 radionazariya107.8@gmail.com	Gujrati, Hindi
35		Junagadh	91.2	Junagadh Janvani	Tel: 285-2672080-90 janvani@jau.in	Gujrati, Hindi
36		Somanath	90.4	Lokvani Radio	Tel: 81283 54453 kvk_junagadh@gmail.com	Gujarati

37		Kutch	90.4	Saiyere Jo Radio	Tel: 02835-221124 ujjasradio@gmail.com	Kutchi
38		Vallabh Vidyanagar	90.4	Vallabh Vidyanagar Campus Radio	Tel: 02692-236545 b_natraj@yahoo.com	Gujrati, English, Hindi
39	Haryana	Ambala	91.2	Mind Tree CRS	Tel: 98880 05254 mindtreeschool@gmail.com	Hindi, English
40		Ellenabad	91.2	RR Radio	Tel: 01698-221477 rrcollegeenb@gmail.com	Hindi, English
41		Faridabad	107.8	Radio Manav Rachna	Tel: 0129-419834 99100 66657 info@radiomanavrachna.com	Hindi, English, Urdu, Pubjabi, Haryanvi
42		Gurgaon	107.8	Gurgaon Ki Awaaz	Tel: 0124-4013645, 98111 26336 info@trfindia.org	Hindi, Haryanvi, Bhojpuri, Maithili
43		Hissar	91.2	CCS Radio	Tel: 94163 97702 jsmalik67@gmail.com	Hindi, Haryanvi
44		Nuh	90.4	Radio Mewat	Tel: 01267-274696 radiomewat90.4@gmail.com	Hindi, Urdu, Mewati
45		Nuh	107.8	Alfaz-e-Mewat	Tel: 98131 64542, 98105 29324 alfazemewat@gmail.com	Mewati, Hindi,Urdu

46		Palwal	90.4	Radio NGF	Tel: 88138 08366 Director_radio@ngfcet.com	Punjabi, Hindi, Haryanvi, English
47		Sirsa	90.4	Radio Sirsa	Tel: 98126 00387 radiosirsa@jansanchaar.in	Hindi, Haryanvi, Bagdi, Rajasthani, Punjabi
48		Sirsa	90.8	JG Radio	Tel: 94161 36006 jgradio568@gmail.com	Hindi, Punjabi, Haryanvi
49		Yamunanagar	90.8	Sanjha Radio	Tel: 89012 95709 sanjharadiocynr@gmail.com	Hindi, Punjabi, English, Urdu, Bhojpuri
50	Himachal Pradesh	Dharmasala	90.4	Tashi Delek FM	Tel: 0189-2220200 manager@tashidelekfm.com	Tibetan
51		Dharmasala	91.2	Radio Gunjan	Tel: 01892-235315 94590 82624 gocd.hp@gmail.com	Hindi, Pahari (Kangri and Gadyali),Dogri, Punjabi, Nepali
52		Solan	90.4	Hamara MSPICM	brijenderpanwar@gmail.com Tel: 01792-229297, 92188 48838 director_mspicm@sify.com	Hindi, Punjabi, Pahari, Bhagati

53		Shimla	90.8	CRS Kuthar	Himachal Harijan Kalyan Sasnsthan Kuthar, Theong, Shimla District 171201	Hindi, Pahari
54	Jammu & Kashmir	Jammu	90.4	Radio Sharda	Tel: 0191-259780 info@radiosharda.com	Kshmiri, Dogri, Punjabi
55	Jharkhand	Garhwa	90.4	Radio Vikalp	Tel: 96319 93190 aidindia@btinternet.com	Hindi, Santali
56		Giridih	90.4	Radio Jagriti	Tel: 94727 20772	Hindi, English, Sanskrit
57		Ranchi	90.4	Radio Khanchi	Ranchi University	Hindi
58			107.8	Radio Birsa Hariyali	www.bauranchi.org/facilities/ other-facilities/	Hindi,
59	Karnataka	Belgavi (Belgaum)	90.8	Nammuru Banlili	Womens Welfare Society, Yellapur Village,Hukkeri Taluk, Belgavi	Kannada
60		Belgavi (Belgaum)	90.4	Venudhwani	Tel: 0831-2472141, 98449 71345 venudhwani@gmail.com	Kannada, Marathi, Urdu, Hindi, English, Konkani
61		Bengaluru	90.4	Radio Active	Tel: 080-22355490, 98458 88686 radioactivecr90.4mhz@gmail.com	Kannada, Tamil, Urdu, English, Telugu

62		Bengaluru	90.4	Ramana Dhawni	Tel: 080-26581076, 9986 444233 mail@srmab.org	Kannada, Hindi
63		Bengaluru Rural	90.4	Sarathi Jhalak	Tel: 98455 36979 shamanthads@gmail.com	Kannada
64		Bengaluru	90.8	Divya Vani Neladhani	Tel: 080-27726066, 94484 67142 lkrishnamurthy@yahoo.com	Kannada
65		Bengaluru	106.8	Radio Universal	Tel: 080-23111020, 98869 89727 radiouniversal.info@gmail.com	Kannada, English, Hindi, Tamil, Telugu
66					Narayana Hrudyalaya School of Nursing	
67		Dharwad	90.4	Krishi CRS	Tel: 0836-2447494, 94484 97356 kcrsuasd@rediffmail.com	Kannada
68		Hubli	90.4	KLE Dhwani	Tel: 0836-2378123 principal@bvb.edu	Kannada, English
69		Kalaburgi (Gulbarga)	90.8	Antarwani	Tel: 08472-263202, 94488 82050 pallaviavp@gmail.com	Kannada, English, Hindi
70		Kolar	90.4	Namma Dhwani	Tel: 08153-256999 98862 61188, nammadhwanicmrc@gmail.com	Kannada, Telugu, Urdu, Tamil

71		Mangaluru (Mangalore)	107.8	Sarang FM	Tel: 0824-2449744, 94485 46425 radiosarang@gmail.com	Konkani, Kannada, Tulu, English, Malayalam, Beary, Hindi, Punjabi
72		Udupi	90.4	Radio Manipal	Tel: 0820-2922747, 94817 5371 radio.manipal@manipal.edu	Kannada, Tulu, Konkani, English
73		Mysuru (Mysore)	90.8	Jana Dhwani	Tel: 96115 39599 janadhwani@svym.org.in	Kannada
74		Puttur	90.8	Radio Panchajanya	Tel: 08251-251223 http://radiopanchajanya.com/	Kannada, English
75		Tumakuru (Tumkur)	90.8	Radio Siddhartha	Tel: 0816-2201342 radiosiddhartha@live.in	Kannada
76		Ujire	90.7	Ninada 90.7	Tel: 08256-236101, 236488 www.sdmcujire.in/	Kannada
77	Kerala	Alappuzha	107.8	Radio Neythal	Tel: 0477- 2255 445 75599 08908 radioneythal@gmail.com	Malayalam
78			91.2	Global Radio	Tel: 0477-2272505, 80866 61912 voiceofalleppey@globalradio.in	Malayalam

79		Changana-cherry	90.8	Radio Media Village	Tel: 0481 2720040, 94477 68033 radiomediavillage90.8@gmail.com	Malayalam, Hindi, English, Tamil
80		Ettumannur	91.2	Radio Mangalam	Tel: 0481-2533722, 2533700, 94950 00780 radio@mangalam.in	Malayalam
81		Karunagapally	91.2	Ente Radio	enteradioindia@gmail.com	Malayalam
82		Kollam	107.8	Radio Benziger	Tel: 0474-2762477, 97447 22299 radiobenziger@gmail.com	Malayalam
83		Mananthavady	90.4	Radio Mattoli	Tel: 04935-242008, 94460 34422 radiomattoli@gmail.com	Malayalam
84		New Mahe	90.8	Janvani	Tel: 0490-2371000, 94463 34656 atedsociety@gmail.com	Malayalam, Hindi, English, Tamil
85		Palakkad	90.4	Ahalia Voice	Tel: 04293-226888 ahailiaradio@gmail.com	Malayalam
86		Thiruvalla	90.4	Radio Macfast	Tel: 0469-3021333 99473 81827 principal@macfast.org	Malayalam, Hindi, English, Tamil
87		Thiruvanan-thapuram	90.4	Radio DC Community FM (Off Air)	Tel: 0471-3942103, 98465 18971 info@radiodcfm.com	Malayalam, English, Hindi

88		Thrissur	90.8	Hello Radio	kidneyfederationofindia@gmail.com	Malayalam
89	Madhya Pradesh	Bhabra	90.4	Vanya Radio Bhabra	Tel: 8305444700 vanya.bhabraradio@gmail.com	Bhili, Hindi
90		Bhopal	90.4	Radio Popcorn	Tel: 0755-4222909 98934 48220 mrityunjaysinghai@yahoo.com	Hindi, English
91		Bhopal	90.8	Radio Azad Hind	Tel: 98262 89379 radioazadhind@gmail.com	Hindi, Urdu, Marathi, Nimadi, Bundeli, Maalvi
92		Bijori	90.4	Bijori Radio	Tel:94246 36097 vanyabijori2213@gmail.com	
93		Chanderi	90.4	Chanderi Ki Awaaz	Tel: 07547-253623, 94257 68634 chanderikiawaaz@gmail.com	Hindi
94		Chandha	90.4	Vanya Radio Chanda	Tel:94246 88881 swilliamsw@yahoo.com	Baigani, Gondi, Hindi
95		Chicholi	90.4	Vanya Radio Chicholi	Tel: 98933 35204 vanya.chicholiradio@gmail.com	Gondi, Hindi
96		Indore			Central India Instt of Science & Technology, M.P.Nagar, Indore	
97		Khalwa	90.4	Vanya Radio Khalwa	Tel: 94245 23908 vanya.khalwaradio@gmail.com	Korku, Hindi

98		Nalcha	90.8	Vanya Radio Nalcha	Tel: 7292280302 vanya.nalchharadio@gmail.com	Hindi, Bhili
99		Jabalpur	90.4	Radio Sanskar	Ashiyana Sanskar Samiti, Aashiyana Sanskar Samiti, F-23, Sainik Society, Shaktinager,Jabalpur 482002	
100		Sheopur	90.8	Vanya Radio Sesaipura	vanya.sesaipuraradio.gmail.com	Saharia, Hindi
101		Sehore	91.2	Radio Awaaz	Tel: 0755-4059369. 91.2mhzfmradioawaaz@gmail.com	Hindi
102		Shivpuri	107.8	Radio Dhadkan	Tel: 0751-2341995, 98109 87257 sambhavshivpuri@gmail.com	Hindi
103		Tikamgarh	90.4	Radio Bundelkhand	Tel: 07680-290951, 94258 13646 radiobundelkhand@devalt.org	Bundeli, Hindi
104		Vidisha	90.4	Kisan Vani	Tel: 07591-253942, 93199 69042 sironjcrs@isapindia.org	Hindi, Malwa, Bundelkhandi
105		Vidisha	90.8	Radio Mann	Tel: 77229 08908 90.8radiomann@gmail.com	
106	Maharashtra	Ahmednagar	90.4	Radio Nagar	Tel: 0241-2321904 98908 32932 radionagar@snehalaya.org	Marathi, English
107		Ahmednagar	90.8	KVK Paravara	Tel: 02422-252414 kvkahmednagar@yahoo.com	Marathi

108		Amravati	90.4	Sadhana Radio	Tel: 0721-2580082 sadhana_crs@yahoo.com	Marathi, Hindi
109		Aurangabad	90.8	MGM Radio	Tel: 0240-6454162, 2480490 mgmjournalism@gmail.com	
110		Baramati	90.4	Vasundhara Vahini	Tel: 02112-239558 , 98817 61891 vasundharacr@gmail.com	Marathi, Hindi
111		Baramati	90.8	Sharada Krishi Vahini	Tel: 02112-255207 kvkbmt@yahoo.com	Marathi
112		Malegaon	90.4	Radio Mast	Tel: 88883 09904 radiomast20july@gmail.com	Marathi, Urdu, Hindi, English,
113		Mumbai	90.4	Dnyan Vani	Tel: 99879 77700 90.4fmdv@gmail.com	Hindi, Marathi, English
114		Mumbai	107.8	MUST Radio (Off Air)	Tel: 022-26525367 98691 64174 radiomust@gmail.com	Marathi, English, Hindi, Gujrati, Tamil
115		Nashik	90.8	Radio Vishwas	Tel:0253-2472626/ 27 radiovishwas@gmail.com	Marathi, English, Hindi
116		Pune	90.4	Radio FTII	Tel: 020-25420 904145, 94230 07993 radioftiioffice@gmail.com	Marathi, Hindi, English
117		Pune	107.4	Vidya Vani	Tel: 020-25690800, 25601278 directorvidyavani@gmail.com	Marathi, Hindi, English

118		Pune	107.8	Puneri Awaz	puneriawazfm@gmail.com	Hindi
119		Sangli	90.4	Green FM	Tel: 0233-2322102 98230 73598 ms.archanagokave@rediffmail.com	Hindi, Marathi
120		Sangli	91.2	Yerala Vani	Tel: 0233-2671318, 94230 29913 yeralavani91.2@gmail.com	Marathi, Kannada
121		Satara	90.4	Mann Deshi Tarang Vahini	Tel: 02373-270400, 94230 33481. manndeshi.mahila@rediffmail.com	Marathi
122		Wardha	90.4	Radio MGIRI	Tel: 07152-253512 director.mgiri@gmail.com	Marathi, Hindi
123		Washim	90.4	Swaranant CRS	Tel: 07251-226511, 99211 74495 swaranantcrs@gmail.com	Marathi
124		Washim	90.8	Radio Vatsa Gulm	Tel: 99700 33445 shoebmadina@rediffmail.com	Marathi, Hindi
125					Lupin Human Welfare and Research Foundation	
126					Shri Hirji Bhojraj & Sons C.V.O. Jain Chhatralaya	
127	Manipur	Imphal	90.4	Radio Loktak	Tel: 76290 00376 radioloktak@gmail.com	
128		Khongjom	91.2	Diamond Radio	Khongjom War Memorial, Khongjom, Kang Samaram	

129	Odisha	Bhadrak	91.2	Radio Bulbul	Tel: 90401 81885 odishadisha@gmail.com	Odiya
130		Bhubaneswar	90.4	Radio 90.4, Voice of the SOA Community	Tel: 0674-2350791 rusi.pattanaik@gmail.com	Odiya, Hindi, Bengali, Telugu, English
131		Bhubaneswar	90.8	AID CRS	Association for Integrated Development, 992-B, Jag Mohan Nagar, Khandgiri, Bhubaneswar-751030	Odiya
132		Cuttack	90.4	Ravenshaw Radio	Tel: 90408 85258 ravenshawradio@gmail.com	Odiya, English, Hindi, Bengali
133		Daspalla	90.4	Radio Surabhi	Tel: 94370 51145 radiosurabhi8@gmail.com	Odiya
134		Jagatsinghpur	91.2	Radio Sanskar	Tel: 06724-220174 98614 06292 radiosanskar@gmail.com	Odiya, Hindi
135		Jajpur	90.2	Radio Swaraj	Tel: 94370 78600 lokbikash@hotmail.com.	Odiya
136		Khurda	90.8	Radio Kissan	Tel: 99381 03885 radiokissanod@yahoo.co.in	Odiya, Hindi
137		Konark	90.4	Radio Namaskar	Tel: 06758-236471, 90409 04904 radionamaskar@gmail.com	Odiya, Telugu, Hindi

138		Koraput	90.4	Radio Dhimsa	Tel: 06852-250590, 94370 77718 sova@sovakoraput.org	Odiya
139		Naupada	90.4	Radio Swayamshakti	Tel: 9437072910, 9040678904	Odiya. Sambalpuri
140		Phulbhani	90.4	Radio Muskan	Tel: 06842-254918 radiomuskan@gmail.com	Odiya
141					Social Association for Dalit Humanity & National Action (SADHANA)	Odiya
142	Puducherry	Puducherry	90.4	NILA FM	Tel: 0413-2640040 (Extn. 230) nila_crs@sify.com	Tamil, English
143		Puducherry	90.8	Honey FM	Tel: 0413-3535999 93600 93675 coordinator@achariya.in	Tamil
144		Puducherry			Sri Aurobindo Society, Puducherry www.aurosociety.org/	
145		Puducherry	107.8	Puduvai Vani	Tel: 0413-2654349, 99767 96865 puduvaivaani@gmail.com	Tamil, English, Hindi, French, Telugu, Bengali, Odiya

146	Punjab	Jalandhar	90.4	Avatar Radio	Tel: 01821-270623 maharaj-ji@nirmakuteya.com	Punjabi
147			90.8	Radio Raabta	Dept. of Journalism & Mass Commn., Doasa College, Jalandhar	
148		Ludhiana	90.4	GNGC CRS	Tel: 0161-2423872 gngoffice@rediffmail.com	
149		Ludhiana	90.8	90.3 FM CR	Tel: 0161-5064800 fmcrs@gndec.ac.in	
150		Patiala	90.8	Khalsa College Radio	Tel: 01887-233908 khalsacollegefm@gmail.com	
151		Patiala	107.8	Radio Chitkara	Tel: 95011 05609 radio1078@chitkara.edu.in	Punjabi, Hindi, English
152		Nawanshahr			Tel: 0182 350 3836	
153	Rajasthan	Ajmer	90.4	Tilonia CRS	Tel: 01463-288210, 99283 76558 tilonia.radio@gmail.com	Marwari, Hindi
154		Alwar	90.8	Alwar Ki Awaz	Tel: 0144-5121190, 95879 09908 radioalwar@gmail.com	Hindi, English
155		Banswara	90.8	Vaagad Community Radio	Tel: 94140 82643 radio@vaagdhara.org	
156		Jaipur	90.4	Radio 7	Tel: 0141-2781154, 97833 00003 fmradio7@icfia.org	Hindi, English

157		Jaipur	91.2	Jayoti Vani	Tel: 01428-515800	
158		Jhunjhunu	90.4	Kamalvani	Tel: 95300 35943 kamalvanicrs@gmail.com	Rajasthani, Hindi, English
159		Mount Abu	90.4	Radio Madhuban	Tel:02974-228888 info@radiomadhuban.in	Rajasthani, Hindi, English
160		Tonk	90.4	Radio Banasthali (Aapno Radio)	Tel: 01438-228432, 228709, 77375 59530 radiobanasthali@gmail.com	Rajasthani, Hindi
161		Tonk	90.4	Radio Eminent	Tel: 0141-240186, 94140 41721 eminentcampus@gmail.com	Hindi, Rajasthani
162					Rajasthan Takniki Prashikshan Sansthan	
163	Tamilnadu	Chennai	90.4	Anna FM	Tel:044-2230010, 97890 72466 arulram@yahoo.com	Tamil, English
164		Chennai	91.2	Thendral CRS	Tel:044-24493772 jeevanalamdana@gmail.com	Tamil
165		Chennai	107.4	Loyola FM	Tel:044-28178200, 98403 08851 loyolafm107.4@gmail.com	Tamil, English
166		Chennai	107.8	MOP FM	Tel: 044-65121333 94440 12043 mopvcfw@eth.net	Tamil
167		Coimbatore	90.8	Rathinavani CR	Tel: 0422- 4040908 82483 03235 mukesh.fm@rathinam.in	Tamil

168		Coimbatore	107.4	Vivasaayi FM	Tel: 0422-6611522, 6611352 dme@tnau.ac.in	Tamil
169		Coimbatore	107.8	PSG CRS	Tel: 0422-4344748, 90038 29486 psgfm@psgtech.ac.in	Tamil, English
170		Cuddalore	107.8	Peridar Kaala Vaanoli - Cuddalore Emeregency Radio	Tel: 04143-231300 80563 35180 saranalayamtrust@rediffmail.com	Tamil
171		Dindigul	90.4	Pasumai FM	Tel: 0451-2461512 pasumaifm@hotmail.com	Tamil
172		Erode	90.4	Kongu CRS	Tel: 04294-220562, 98431 21359 kongucrs@kongu.ac.in	Tamil
173		Erode	91.2	Mugil FM	Tel: 04294-232701 www.erode-sengunthar.ac.in/?page_id=381	Tamil
174		Kalpakkam	90.8	Kalpakkam CRS	Tel: 044-27487800, 94425 23825 aecskal2@yahoo.co.in	Tamil, English
175		Kanchipuram	90.8	Sruthi FM	Sri Sankara Arts & Science College, Enathur, Kacnchipuram-631561 http://sankaracollege.edu.in/	Tamil

176		Karur	91.2	MKC CRS	Tel: 04324-272155 manager@mkce.ac.in	Tamil
177		Kattankual-thur	90.4	Muthucharam CRS	Tel: 94862 57028 cr.muthucharam@gmail.com	Tamil, English
178		Kongana-puram	91.2	AGN School CRS	Tel: 04283-265488 office.agncrs@gmail.com	Tamil, English
179		Kotagiri	90.4	Radio Kotagiri	Tel: 04266-271977 radio@keystone-foundation.org	Tamil, English
180		Madurai	90.4	Vayalaga Vanoli	Tel: 04544-230485 99448 28346 vayalagavanoli@gmail.com	Tamil
181		Madurai	90.4	Shyamalavani CRS	Tel: 0452-3918609, 98947 27999 rip@dinamalar.in	Tamil, English, Hindi
182		Madurai	91.2	PARD Vanoli	Tel: 0452-253349 pardmadurai@hotmail.com	Tamil
183		Nagapattinam	90.8	Kalanjiam Samuga Vanoli	Tel: 04365 - 268606, 90422 71293 kalanjiamvanoli@gmail.com	Tamil
184		Namakkal	90.8	PGP Radio	Tel: 04286-267919 98408 32578 pgpcrs@gmail.com	Tamil, English
185		Namakkal	90.8	SSM CRS	Tel: 99526 70221, 98947 04992 crs@ssmce.ac.in	Tamil, English
186		Nammakal	91.2	Namakkal KVK CR	Krishi Vigyan Kendra, Namakkal	Tamil

187		Rameswaram	90.4	Kadalosai	Nesakarangal Trust, Rameswaram	Tamil
188		Satyaman-galam	90.4	Bannari Amman CR	Bannari Amman Institute of Technology, Satyamangalam, Gobichettipalayam	Tamil
189		Sriperum-bedur	107.2	Ilanthalir CRS	Tel: 044-27162128 ahdproject@gmail.com	Tamil
190		Thanjavur	90.4	Periyar CRS	Tel: 04362-264600 99444 95670 periyarcr@yahoo.in	Tamil
191		Thanjavur	91.2	Valar Thamizh Vanoli	Tel: 04362- 227040 tamilunivc@gmail.com	Tamil
192		Tiruchengode	90.4	KSR CRS	Tel: 04288-274996 98847 39009 ksrcr904@gmail.com	Tamil, English
193		Tiruchendur	90.4	Sivanthi CRS	Tel: 04639 245175, 94863 91546 isehar_9307@yahoo.co.in	Tamil, English
194		Tiruchirapalli	90.4	Holy Cross CRS	Tel: 78711 19787 holycross_communityradio@yahoo.com	Tamil
195		Tiruchirapalli	90.8	NITT Radio FM	Tel: 0431-2503000 crsfm90.8@nitt.edu	Tamil
196		Vellore	90.8	VIT CR	Tel: 0416-2204400, 99444 41196 vitcr@vit.ac.in	Tamil, English, Hindi, Telugu

197					Imam Shafi (RAM) Matriculation Higher Secondary School	Tamil
198		Villupuram	90.4	BWDA CR	Tel: 04146-242904, 99944 72173 bwdacrs@bwda.org.in	Tamil
199	Telangana	Hyderabad	90.4	Bol Hyderabad	Tel: 040-23135505, 93943 15787 bolhyd90.4@gmail.com	Telugu, English, Hindi, Urdu
200		Hyderabad	90.4	KMIT Tarang (Off Air)	Tel: 040-23263408, 98491 59679 abhisheka@kmit.in	Hindi, Telugu, English
201		Hyderabad	90.4	Pragnya Community Radio	Tel: 040 68566 4440 98490 39569 pragnyafm@griet/ac/in	Hindi, Telugu, English
202		Hyderabad		CGC Radio	Child Guidance Centre, 7-6/2, Santosh Sadan, Near Ganesh Nagar, Peerzadiguda, Hyderabad -500039 cgcguidencecentre@rediffmail.com	Telugu
203		Hyderabad	107.8	Deccan Radio (Off Air)	Tel: 98482 56515, 92463 65401 deccanradio107.8mhz@gmail.com	Urdu, English, Telugu, Hindi

204		Hyderabad	107.8	Radio Charminar	Tel: 040--24511078, 24511079 www.radiocharminar.com/	Urdu
205		Khammam	90.4	KLR Radio	Tel: 8744-253636 klrpaloncha@gmail.com	Telugu
206		Kodad	90.4	Radio Guru	Integrated Development Organisation, Kodad, Nalgonda	Telugu
207		Medak	90.4	Sangham Radio	Tel: 08451-282271 sateeshperiyapatna@gmail.com	Telugu
208	Tripura	Agartala	90.4	Friends FM	Tel:0381-2511111, 76289 53430 crsprojecttripura@gmail.com	Bangla
209	Uttar Pradesh	Agra	90.4	Agra Ki Awaaz	Tel: 98376 63707 agrakiawaz@gmail.com	Hindi, Brij and Khadi Boli
210		Agra	90.8	Aap Ki Awaaz	Tel: 93681 23457, 75000 6000 aapkiawazfm@gmail.com	Hindi, English
211		Aligarh	90.8	FM Alive	Tel: 92505 83308 wada1988@gmail.com	Hindi, English
212		Allahabad	90.4	Radio Adan	Tel: 94153 16348 radioadan90.4crs@yahoo.com	Hindi, Bhjpuri
213		Azamgarh	90.8	Voice of Azamgarh	Tel: 98392 11624 www.voiceofazamgarh.com	Hindi, English, Urdu
214		Basti	90.4	Kisan Radio	Tel: 94151 73162 kisan.fm@gmail.com kss.org@gmail.com	Hindi, Bhojpuri

215		Faizabad	90.4	-	Narendra Dev Agriculture University, Faizabad	
216		Ghaziabad	90.4	HINT FM	Tel: 0120-2710226, 98101 39911 hintradio90.4@gmail.com	Hindi
217		Ghazipur	90.4	Ghazipur CRS	Tel: 0548- 2220045 teripgc@rediffmail.com	Hindi, Bhojpuri
218		Gorakhpur			Carvan Sanskritik Evam Vikas Manch, Gorakhpur www.saathire.com/2EE/carvan-sanskritik-evam-vikas-manch/	
219		Gorakhpur	90.8	Radio Gorakhpur	Tel: 94150 10554 radiogorakhpur90.8@gmail.com	
220		Kanpur	90.4	IIT Kanpur CRS	Tel: 0512-2594479 94157 59394 90.4@iitk.ac.in	Hindi, English
221		Kanpur	91.2	Waqt Ki Awaaz	Tel: 0512-2581091, 2580823 waqtkiawaaz@gmail.com	Hindi
222		Lalitpur	90.4	Lalit Lokvani	Tel: 05176- 282675, 96489 39943 lalitlokvani@gmail.com	Bundelkhandi, Hindi
223		Lucknow	90.4	CMS Radio	Tel: 0522-2638738, 94150 15039 cmsfm@cmseducation.org	Hindi
224		Lucknow	90.4	CMS DC Radio	Tel: 0522-2435690, 94150 15039 vkurian@csmeducation.org	Hindi

225		Lucknow	90.8	BBD 90.8	Tel: 90052 33333 bbdcrs90.8@gmail.com	Hindi, Awadhi, Bhojpuri, English
226		Meerut	90.4	Radio IIMT	Tel: 0121-2622263, 98080 63822 director_radio@iimtindia.net	Hindi
227		Muzzafarpur	90.8	Radio SD	Tel: 89370 95000 radiosd90.8fm@gmail.com radiosdfm.com	
228		Noida	90.4	Salaam Namaste	Tel: 0120-4798888, 97174 11111 info@salaamnamaste.in	Hindi, English, Haryanvi, Punjabi, Bhojpuri, Bengali, Garhwali, Assamese, Sindhi, Tamil.
229		Noida	91.2		National Institute of Open School, Noida	
230		Noida	107.4	Radio Noida	Tel: 0120-2515254, 99685 43245 info@radionoida.fm	Hindi, Bhojpuri, Kaurvi (Haryanavi/ Goojari) English

231		Noida	107.8	Radio Amity	Tel: 0120-4392297, 99583 61401 radioamity107.8fm@gmail.com	Hindi, English
232		Greater Noida	90.8	Suno Sharda	Tel: 0120-4570000 www.sharda.ac.in/suno-sharda	
233		Greater Noida	91.2	Radio Lok Manch	Tel: 0120-2517337 radionoidalokmanch@gmail.com	
234		Saharanpur	90.4	Vallabh Kriishak Radio	Tel: 0132-2664480, 94110 78115 kvksaharanpur01@gmail.com	
235	Uttarakhand	Chamba	90.4	Hevalvaani Samudayik Radio	Tel: 01376-256159 Tel. 94129 70251 henvalvanicr@gmail.com	Garhwali, Kumauri, Jaunshari, Hindi
236		Dehradun	90.8	Radio Zindagee	Tel: 80573 51062 radiozindagee@gmail.com	Hindi
237		Dehradun	91.2	NIVH Hello Doon	Tel: 0135-274449 director@nivh.org.in	Hindi, English, Garhwali
238		Dehradun	107.8	Himagiri Ki Awaaz	Tel: 0135-2760464 himgirizeeuniversity@gmail.com	Hindi, English
239		Haldwani	91.2	Hello Haldwani	Tel: 05946286021 94109 64787crs@uou.ac.in	Hindi, English, Kumaoni, Garhwali

240		Mussoorie	90.4	Radio Khushi	Tel: 0135-2632637, 99279 94633 radiokhushi@yahoo.co.in	Hindi, English Garhwali, Kumaoni, Punjabi, Jaunpuri.
241		Nainital	90.4	Kumaon Vani	Tel: 011-2468 2100, 95364 76660 kumaonvani@gmail.com	Hindi, Kumaoni
242		Pantnagar	90.8	Pantnagar Janvani	Tel: 05944-233122, 94123 64276 pantnagar_janvani@rediffmail.com	Hindi
243		Rudra Parayag	90.8	Mandakini Ki Awaz	Tel: 98370 95433 radiomandakini@gmail.com	Hindi
244	West Bengal	Darjeeling	90.8	Radio Salesian	Tel: 79080 74156 radiosalesian@gmail.com	Nepalese, Bengali, English
245		Jhargram	90.4	Radio MIlan	Tel: 03321-255903 www.highmediaindia.com	Santhali, Bengali
246		Kolkata	90.4	Radio SRFTI	Tel: 033-24329875, 98364 09379 srfticommunityradio@gmail.com	Bengali, Hindi, English
247		Kolkata	90.8	JU Radio	Tel: 033-2414 6060, 2414 6362 radioju@gmail.com	Bengali, Hindi, English
248		Kolkata	91.2	Y FM	Tel: 033-2403 0154 nshmradio@nshm.com	Bengali, Hindi, English

249		Medinipur	91.2	Palli Bangla FM Radio	Tel: 80013 40888 / 78726 50969 pallibangla91.2@gmail.com	Bengali
250		Purlia	91.2	Nityananda Janavani	Tel: 03253-259 504 9732167160 purulia@mant.org.in	Bengali, Santhali

List of operational Community Radio Stations as on 23 Aug 2018 published by Ministry of Information & Broadcasting, Government of India

Compiled by Jose Jacob, VU2JOS, National Institute of Amateur Radio, Hyderabad, India, updated by CRA

Annexure 4 : Community Radio Map of India

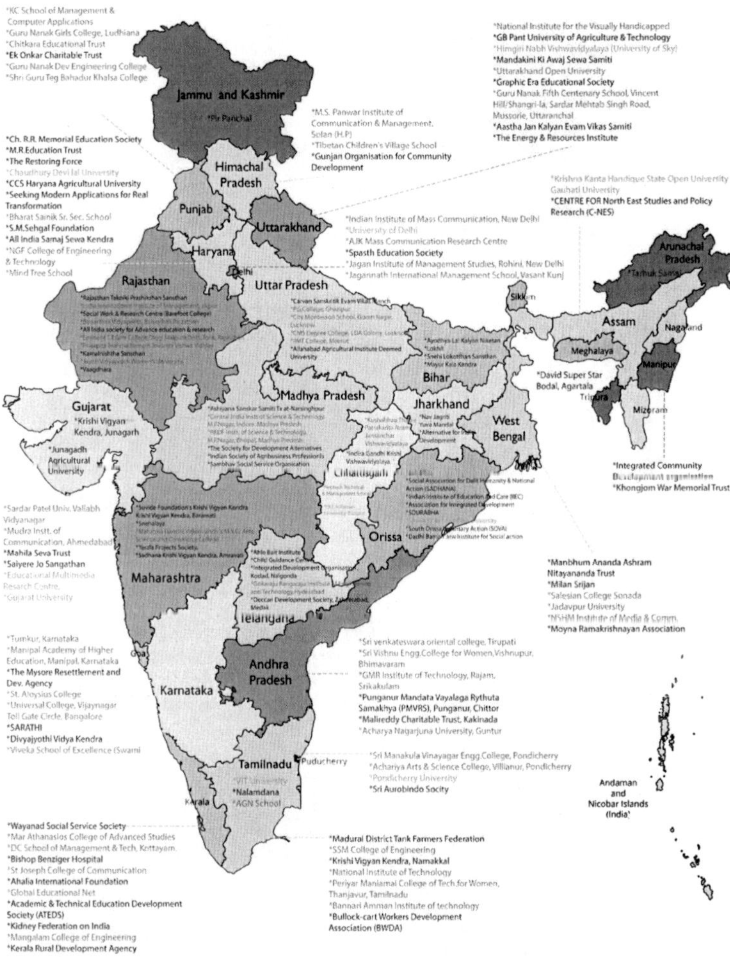

(As of November 2018, purely for representative purposes only and does not represent geographical or political boundaries)

Map by: Satish Nagaraji

Annexure 5 : Pictures

The CR Application/Licensing Process

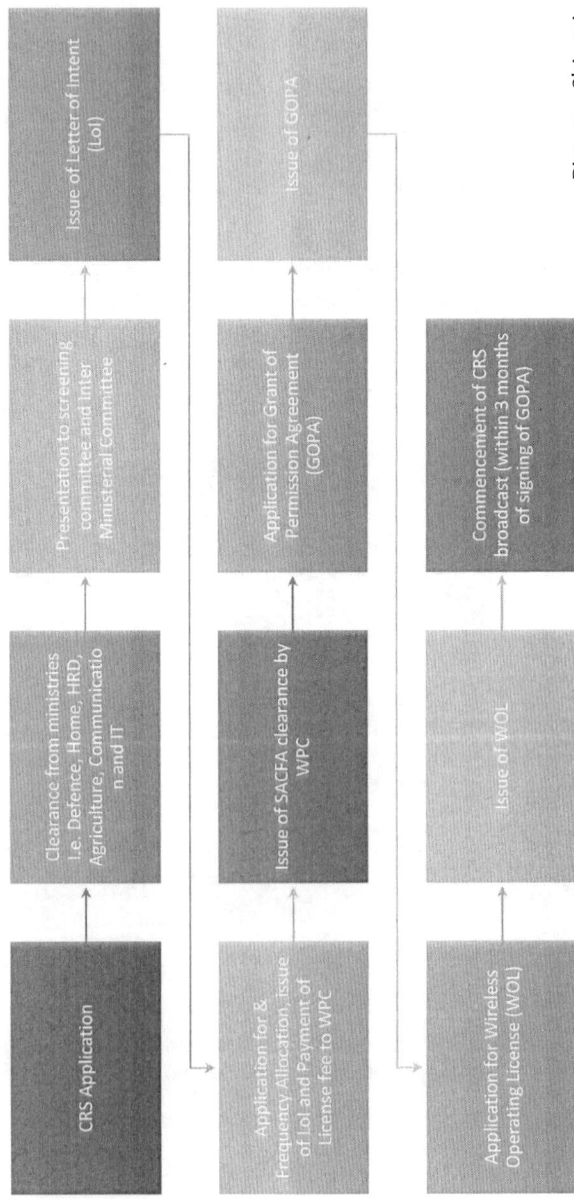

Picture : Shivani

View of Studio

Radio Tower and Antenna

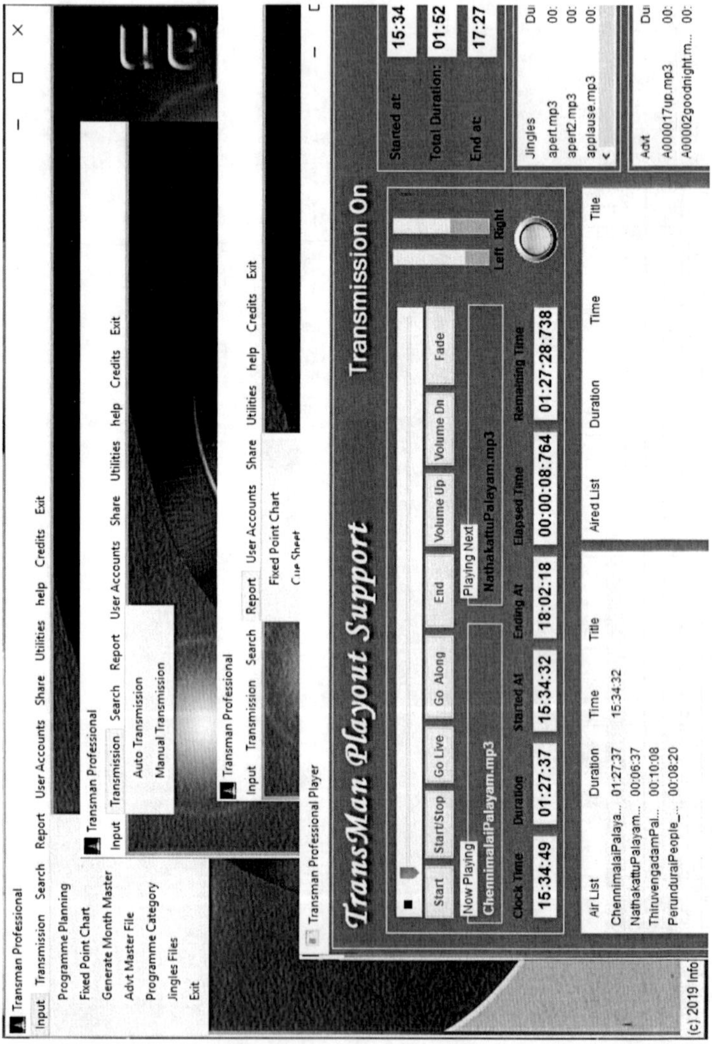

Transmission Automation (courtesy: V. Krishnamoorthy)

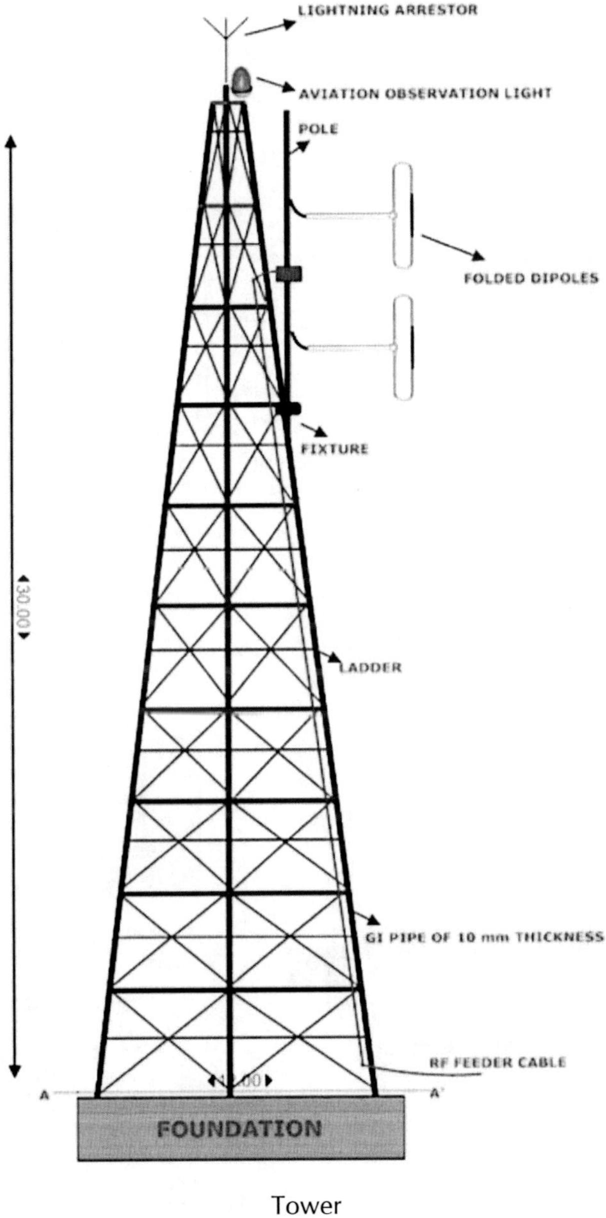

Tower

Picture : Broadcast Engineering Consultants India Ltd. (BECIL)

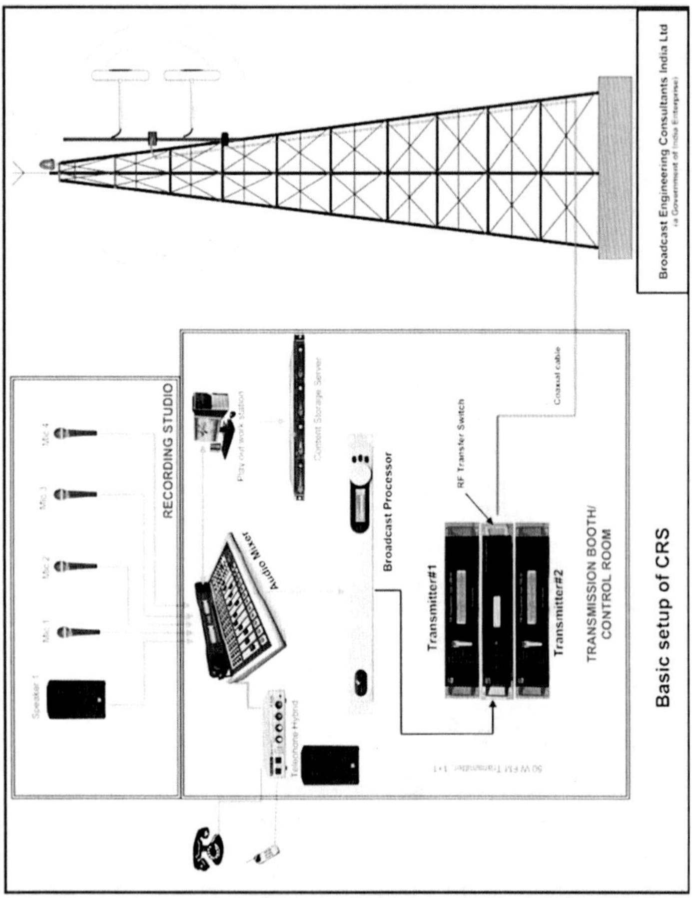
Broadcast Engineering Consultants India Ltd
RECORDING STUDIO
Audio Mixer
Broadcast Processor
RF Transfer Switch
Coaxial cable
Transmitter#1
Transmitter#2
TRANSMISSION BOOTH/
CONTROL ROOM
Basic setup of CRS

Radio Listeners (courtesy: Al-Amin Yusuph)

Studio

Community Radio Anchor

Community Radio Anchor

Group Discussion

Listeners

Community Broadcasters in Studio

Control Room (Live Broadcast)

Field Recording

Studio Discussion

Acknowledgements

The authors thank Prof. K.G. Suresh, the Director General of Indian Institute of Mass Communication, faculty and the publication division for having encouraged us to write a book and carried out along the road. Thanks are due to the Sehgal Foundation for their trust on the co-author Ms. Pooja O. Murada and for giving her all the support to start and practice community radio along with the rural community of district Nuh, Haryana. Grateful thanks are due to Mr. Satish Nagaraji, presently at ICRISAT Hyderabad for his work on the updated CR Map of india and other illustrations. The authors are grateful for the excellent support given by Ms. Arti Grover of the Sehgal Foundation for her help in preparing the manuscript. Assistance given by Ms. Ishita Pradhan, the then Intern at Commonwealth Educational Media Centre for Asia. Ms. Marly Cornell's help with her very professional editing inputs in making the document print worthy is to be appreciated specially. Special thanks to Mr. Anirban Sarma, National Programme Officer, Communication and Information Sector at UNESCO for his support. Dr. Sreedher also would like to thank Prof. Asha Kanwar President of Commonwealth of Learning for permitting him to support the CR movement in Asia during his tenure as Director of Commonwealth Educational Media Centre for Asia which in turn facilitated him with a vast experience in the field. Thanks are also due to Dr. Shahid Rasool, Director, CEMCA and his colleagues with special mention to Ms. Monica Sharma. Authors also thank Prof. Vinay Shanker of IP University, Delhi and Ms. Shirley Deepak, formerly from Holy Cross College for their meticulous vetting of the manuscript. A special mention must be made to Ms. Priyadarshini Kiran, Assistant Professor, School of Journalism, Teerthanker Mahaveer University, Moradabad for her help in running the manuscript on "Tune it in" software for plagiarism.

The Government of India and particularly the Ministry of Information and Broadcasting needs a very special mention without whose policies the Community Radio Movement would not have been possible and so is this publication.

Community Radio sector as a whole is indebted to UNESCO for steering it across the globe and the authors thank Mr. Eric Falt, Director UNESCO South Asia and Mr. Al-Amin Yusuph, its Communication Advisor and Community Radio Practitioners for their support and forward to this book.

Dr. R. Sreedher is Professor Emeritus at Apeejay Stya University, Sohna, Delhi, and is the past Director of Commonwealth Educational Media Centre for Asia (CEMCA). He has worked with electronic media since 1972. He joined All India Radio as Assistant Editor for Science Reporting in 1976. He was Producer of Spoken Word at AIR Coimbatore, a Science Officer of AIR Chennai (1980-87), Director of Programmes Education at Delhi (1988-1993), Dy Director of Staff Training, Dy Director of Sports, Director of Farm and Home, and Station Director at All India Radio Bhopal (1996-98). He was a member of the Innovation Sub Council for Media innovation for Government of India and the committee for restructuring Prasar Bharati, both headed by Sam Pitroda. He was one of three experts on the Technical Expert committee formed to advise the Prasar Bharati Board on all matters relating to All India Radio and Doordarshan (2012-14). He is credited with launching DD movie channel and DD Bangla channel and was personally involved in launching Gyan Darshan and GyanVani Educational Television and FM Channels through IGNOU. Before leaving IGNOU, he had the distinction of launching fourteen radio channels and four TV channels. As a consultant for UNESCO, he revamped the Educational Media Centre in Afghanistan. Dr. Sreedher has been associated with the Community Radio Movement from its inception and played a role in forming its original as well as revised policies, motivating more than 150 of the 238 stations by October 2018. He was responsible for the launch of India's first community radio station in Anna University Chennai. Widely traveling to more than twenty countries, he served as consultant to UNESCO, UNICEF, and Commonwealth of Learning in matters of educational media. He worked as director of Educational Media Centres at IGNOU (1998-2003), Anna University (2003-05), and IIT Roorkee (2005-06). He was a finalist for a World Technology Network Award for Education in 2002 and a selected Fellow of WTN. He received the Government of India National Award for Science Popularisation in 1991 and won four Akashvani National Awards for Innovative Radio Production. He was syndicate member of Tamil Nadu Open University and held several positions in Research Councils of CSIR, governing bodies of the National Institute of Open Schooling, Consortium of Educational Communication, UGC, Indian Institute of Mass Communication, Vigyan Prasar, on multiple university academic councils and study boards, and as visiting faculty at educational institutions in India and other countries.

Email: r.sreedher@gmail.com Phone +919810778459

Pooja O. Murada is the director, Communications at S M Sehgal Foundation and founder and representative of Community radio Alfaz-e- Mewat FM 107.8. She has served as the chairperson of the Gender Committee at Sehgal Foundation since 2017. She has held honorary advisory positions for Community Radio-IGNOU, India Development Coalition of America, and Community Radio Association; and served as an invited external committee member for C P Wholesale India Pvt. Ltd., and as guest faculty at the YMCA School of Media Studies in Delhi and on the editorial board of *Schoolmantra Magazine*.

Pooja has worked for more than twenty years in brand management, marketing communications, and communications for development, with more than a decade in the area of marketing and corporate communications for multinationals. In her ten-plus years working in the development sector, she has raised issues about the information divide at the grassroots and shared best practices for bridging those divides at various forums. Her writing has been to build awareness of various social causes, and her articles and papers have been published in professional journals and other print and online publications.

To bridge the large information divide in the rural areas, she uses a variety of media communications and ICT channels including community media such as street theatre, wall painting, community newspapers and broadcasting mediums. In her work with S M Sehgal Foundation she started a community radio station in 2012 in one of the aspirational districts (as stated by Niti aayog) in Nagina Block of district Nuh (Mewat). Community Radio *Alfaz-e-Mewa*t is broadcast on FM 107.8 megahertz. The station's programming reaches 225 villages in Nuh and to many more with narrow and web casting. Thirteen hours of daily programming on Alfaz-e-Mewat is carried out through participatory content development, and the local villagers are trained to run the radio station and produce the content.

Pooja has served as a governing board member of Community Radio Association for two years, and currently nominated as an advisor to the association.

Email: Pooja.murada@gmail.com